"This is a fascinating collection of supplications, praises, and prayers that rings eloquently and hauntingly with enchanting images, symbolisms, and the natural worldview of Africa. The earthy and ecological renditions serve as a reminder of the rich soil of African religious cosmology in which Christianity continues to nourish its Christology, pneumatology, and spirituality. . . . But the context of Afua Kuma offers valuable resources for appreciating Christianity's long march to inculturation in Africa."

—AGBONKHIANMEGHE OROBATOR,
SJ, author of Religion and Faith in Africa

"*The Surprising African Jesus* is a real treasure. Afua Kuma's prayers are powerful, sometimes violent, but at other times deeply heartfelt, tender, and beautiful. I couldn't help thinking, as I was rereading them, that they make up a genuine African psalter . . . . Readers can only be grateful for Jon's beautiful, rhythmic translation, but especially for Afua's vivid African imagination and shining faith."

—STEPHEN BEVANS,
SVD, Catholic Theological Union, emeritus

"Afua Kuma's prayers will endorse for African Christians the ongoing effort to find Jesus in their own environments and to not be ashamed to converse with him in their own languages, born of their own observations and experiences along the path of life. For the rest of the (Christian) world, the value lies in empathy understood as 'fellow feeling' and expanded wisdom."

—LAURENTI MAGESA,
Jesuit School of Theology, Hekima University College

"I recommend this book very highly as the witness of an amazing African woman whose voice is unmatched in contemporary theology. Theologians, scholars of African Christianity, and students of women and religion will welcome this remarkable volume with awe and gratitude. Kirby and his partners deserve hearty thanks for making it widely available."

—DANA L ROBERT,
Boston University School of Theology

"In this new collection of Afua Kuma's prayers and praises lies a treasure trove of good things, especially the glimpse into the arresting and vibrant spirituality of a woman 'grassroots' theologian in love with Jesus, which is both deeply African and deeply Christian. We are indebted to Jon Kirby for this labor of love in once again making her prayers and praises accessible to a wider audience."

—GILLIAN MARY BEDIAKO,
Akrofi-Christaller Institute

"As all who have read *Jesus of the Deep Forest* (1981) know, the prayers and praises of Afua Kuma are a gift to the worldwide church. Now, in *The Surprising African Jesus*, the 'grassroots' voice of West African Christianity once again springs to life on each page through words and images that will draw readers into the experience of faith with a freshness and vitality seldom expressed."

—JEFFREY W. BARBEAU,
Wheaton College

THE SURPRISING AFRICAN JESUS

THE SURPRISING AFRICAN JESUS

The Lost Prayers and Praises of Afua Kuma

AFUA KUMA

Translated by Jon P. Kirby
&
Transcribed by Joseph Kwakye

WIPF & STOCK · Eugene, Oregon

THE SURPRISING AFRICAN JESUS
The Lost Prayers and Praises of Afua Kuma

Wipf & Stock
An Imprint of Wipf and Stock Publishers
199 W. 8th Ave., Suite 3
Eugene, OR 97401

www.wipfandstock.com

PAPERBACK ISBN: 978-1-6667-3098-2
HARDCOVER ISBN: 978-1-6667-2300-7
EBOOK ISBN: 978-1-6667-2301-4

FEBRUARY 17, 2022 2:35 PM

To the memory of Afua Kuma (1908–87)—sketch by Mark Shaw.

"I am a Ghanaian from Kwahu-Obo. My full name is Christiana Gyane. My other name is Afua Kuma. My father's name is Albert Omari. He was a senior presbyter in the Presbyterian Church. He has long gone to his maker. Elizabeth Nartey Somuaa is my daughter. Her husband is Pastor Nartey. He is the senior pastor in the Church of Pentecost. I stay in Obo. One other town where they can find me is Asempaneye or Atuobikurom."

Contents

Permissions

- The watercolor sketch of Afua Kuma is used with permission of the artist, Mark Shaw.
- The following are used with permission from Rex Vegbey, SVD:

    2.   They were waving white handkerchiefs in praise.

    20.   "Great chiefs are going before him."

    35.   "Precious gifts for our young Savior."

    48.   "I will follow the priests, who take the lead in processions."

    55.   "You are the Treasures of Women."

- The two photographs of artwork are used with the permission of Rosemary Keatley:

    7.   "Sun and . . . rain make use of their powers in vain."

    81.   "Jesus, you are the Mighty Tree."

- Seven photographs belong to the author, Jon P. Kirby:

    1.   Weaving a strip of kente on a traditional loom.

    24.   "His is the food that satisfies."

    27.   "We have taken our holy baths."

    59.   "Fishing nets . . . spanned the sea from east to west."

    86.   "Before you reach that inner door."

    88.   "Jesus, you are the Deep Forest."

    96.   "Like dancing kings at a durbar."

- Eleven photographs are licensed to Jon P. Kirby by AdobeStock:

  16.   "He, the Strongest of Fetishes."

  22.   "The thick *Sakyi* fog surrounds us."

  51.   "You are the precious Kente Cloth."

  57.   "He was standing there on the sea performing . . . wonders."

  62.   "You will burn like a piece of roasted plantain."

  72.   "If you go to drink of this Font, everlasting life will be yours."

  77.   "A green mamba was there to meet them."

  89.   "You are the Greatest of Rivers."

  91.   "Of fishermen kin, I have none."

  93.   "Jesus, the Sea Hawk, hooks our fish."

  98.   "Jesus' touch is like a cannon."

All the other photographs are from the Foto Bank Archive of the Society of the Divine Word (SVD), Missionari Verbiti, Via dei Verbiti 1, 00154 Roma, Italia (http://svdcuria.org/members/communic/fotobank/index.htm), or the Africa Fotos (AF) of the Photo Mission World (http://www.svdphotos.org/) collected by the Mission Secretary of POL, © 2015–2021 SVD. I am a member of the SVD, and these photos are available to use for publications free of charge by any member of the Society. The names of the persons who contributed the actual photos are indicated next to each photo. They have given their permission to the SVD for any member to use the photos.

List of Images

Foreword

IN 1996, I HAD THE PRIVILEGE of accompanying a number of students from Catholic Theological Union, Lutheran School of Theology, and McCormick Theological Seminary—all here in Chicago—on a three-week study trip to Ghana, West Africa. Our host in those weeks was my longtime friend and Society of the Divine Word (SVD) brother Jon Kirby, director of the Tamale Institute of Cross-Cultural Studies (TICCS), located in the city of Tamale in the northern part of the country. Jon, the editor and commentator of this volume, is the founder of TICCS and was a veteran missionary in Ghana, a master of several of its languages, and a lover of its culture. After several years in Ghana, Jon enrolled in the University of Cambridge and earned a doctorate in anthropology under the eminent anthropologist Jack Goody so as to be even more effective in his missionary work.

The three weeks in Ghana were for me a truly unforgettable time. During the first week, Jon would lecture us in the morning on Ghanaian history and culture, and in the afternoon, we would travel to various sites in the area: visiting a chief and his court, a local tannery, a hospital built in such a way that patients were never separated from their families, a local diviner. The day after we arrived, we visited the fortress at Elmina that was used to hold enslaved women, men, and children for the infamous voyage to Europe and the Americas. One of our number, an African American woman, said that she could smell the unwashed and brutalized bodies of the women and men once imprisoned there. In our second week, we began to study the local language, Dagbanli, and to practice it with people around the Institute and in Tamale itself. We had no hope of learning the language well, of course, but the effort brought us into contact with real people in the streets, taxis, and marketplaces of the town. One Sunday, we attended a celebration at the Tamale cathedral that was filled with music and danc-ing in the way only Africans can celebrate. A lasting image was the aged archbishop, Peter Poreku Dery, dancing around the altar as he incensed it at the preparation of the gifts. The highlight of our time at TICCS was spending three days in a local village and meeting the people, eating their food, and being guided by a member of the village who was steeped in local culture and local wisdom.

I can't remember exactly when it was—perhaps one evening sipping local beer in the Institute's roof garden—when Jon showed me a slim, rather poorly printed volume he had edited entitled *Jesus of the Deep Forest* by Afua Kuma, the author of this collection as well.

It was stunning. For some twenty years, I had been interested in contextual theology, and several years before coming to Ghana on this trip, I had published *Models of Contextual Theology*,[1] a book in which I tried to map the landscape of contextual theology through the lens of five (in a second edition, six) models. These models ranged from *translating* the Christian message *into* local contexts and cultures to *recognizing* that message within those very contexts and cultures—as Jon put it in one of his classes, from "putting the gospel *into* the culture" to "pulling it *out* of a culture."

One of the things that I insisted upon in my book was that the local people—not the missionaries, and sometimes not even the local church leaders—should be the ones to enculturate the gospel. Rather, the local people, often the simplest of people, should be the ones to express the gospel in the local idiom. This is what Jon Kirby and his SVD associates discovered in the prayers of Afua Kuma, both in the volume that I first saw in 1996 and then in this present work, rescued from a dusty box of long-forgotten cassette tapes recorded in the 1970s. The prayers and praises on those tapes come out of a different world from that of Western religion or Western theology; they truly reveal "the surprising African Jesus," as this book is entitled. They come also from a woman of deep faith who had a phenomenal grasp of the local language, Twi, as Jon attests in his introduction. They are powerful, sometimes violent, but at other times deeply heartfelt, tender, and beautiful. I couldn't help thinking, as I was rereading them just before writing this foreword, that they make up a genuine African psalter, with all the emotions that the biblical Psalter gives us. Afua Kuma exalts Jesus as the great hunter, the expert marksman; she rails against her enemies, especially the devil, and she praises Jesus as one with the local landscape. The prayers are studded with colorful and mind-expanding imagery. For example, she writes:

1. Bevans, *Models of Contextual Theology*.

You are the precious Kente Cloth
    and the colorful Dutch Wax Prints.
You brighten our celebrations.
    We marvel at your majesty.
The fame of your splendor has spread.
    All the world has come to know you.
They all admire your beauty.
    You are the wonderful Silk Scarf,
which we use to cover our heads.
    You are the Unbreakable Stone,
which cannot be smote by a fist.
    You are the Violent River,
which one cannot blockade with sand.
    You are the Powerful River,
which no bar of sand can oppose.
    You are Lord of Travelers!
Your gospel reaches every land.

Time and again, Afua calls to mind how Jesus saved her in language that transcends her local context and yet gets its power and beauty from it:

But he has tied his cloth to mine
    and lifted the weight off my chest.
These things weighed heavily on me.
    I have carried them on my back.
But he has tied his cloth to mine
    and has taken them off my back.

Many passages seem to paraphrase Scripture but do it in a fully African way. Jesus' eucharistic discourse in chapter 6 of John's gospel, for example, might come to mind when we read Afua's call to:

Bring your empty stomachs to him
    and let them be filled with his fare.
He tells his children not to cry;
    to come for their meat and be filled—
the meat of the young wild bull!

While the missionary or theologian is not the one to articulate a local, contextual theology, she or he does have a crucial role to play in its development, at least at times. That role is to be a *midwife*—one who assists in the birth of a theological and pastoral expression of Christianity that is rooted in the soil of a particular people, time, or experience but offers new and fresh ways of imagining the gospel that enriches the entire church.

This is what Jon Kirby has done with his passion to bring the prayers and praises of Afua Kuma to a wider readership. Readers can only be grateful for Jon's beautiful, rhythmic translation, but especially for Afua's vivid African imagination and shining faith.

Stephen Bevans, SVD

Preface

BEFORE PRESENTING THIS COMPLETELY new collection of the prayers and praises of Afua Kuma (whose name means "second/the lesser Friday born"), I would like to offer some background to the first project, *Jesus of the Deep Forest*. This is to offer the introductory information that was lacking in the original publication but which sets the scene for this second project.

I begin with my memory of the first momentous meeting with Afua Kuma that day in 1976 when I was travelling by "moto" up-country from Accra to my mission station in the north. After a few backbreaking hours on the road, I stopped for a short break along the way and met with a friend who ushered me over to a nearby hospital to witness, as he put it, "something very wonderful." He led me into a long, open ward where there were beds lined against walls interspersed with mosquito-screen windows. Down the middle was a long corridor. As we walked along, my attention was drawn to a large crowd at the end of the ward from which I heard a rhythmic narration in the local language, Twi. All the faces in the ward were turned in that direction.

When we reached the spot and gently pushed through the group to see what was happening, I suddenly realized I was surrounded by the visiting friends and relatives of the patients. Alongside them were stethoscope-draped doctors and nurses with charts in their hands. My mind was spinning. What made them leave their relatives and patients? What was this reverberating sound that was able draw them here and command such rapt attention? The answer came quickly. It was something that neither I nor—from the looks on their faces—anyone present could ever have heard or seen before. Standing there, hovering over a patient in the corner, was a diminutive woman with the assured faith and conviction of a Ghanaian John the Baptist. Clickety-click, clickety-clack. With machine-gun cadence and boundless energy, a great stream of royal Asante lore, complete with proverbs and other oral art, poured from her lips. But what made this high-level verbal cascade especially marvelous was the fact that it was in the form of prayers and praises to Jesus. It was high Akan culture harnessed to the work of the Lord. At that time, I had almost native fluency in the Twi language, but I had never heard anything like this before. And clearly, from all the jaw dropping and rapt attention, I could see that neither had anyone else.

I thought to myself that this was a missionary's eureka moment! I had stumbled upon something of the greatest significance for African Christianity—indeed, for Christianity itself. It was the kind of missiological Rosetta Stone that unlocks the African religious psyche which, as a budding missionary-anthropologist, I had been longing to see and hear. I immediately knew that this was something that needed to find its way into the hands, minds, and hearts of the people. It was infinitely more important than all the translations of catechisms, prayer books, and rituals that I and some of my colleagues had been laboring over. It bypassed all those fought-over European-culture-based denominational differences by reaching to the very heart of the peoples' religiosity. Instantly, all my other duties and obligations were pushed back. There was only one great task before me now: getting this woman's praises into print. With this uppermost in mind, and with a set of her precious cassette-tape recordings in my bag, I happily continued on my way. I hardly noticed the next four hundred miles of washed-out, pot-holed, and gravelly roads to Chereponi, north of Yendi. All I could think of was Afua Kuma.

Over the next few years, more recordings were made of Afua at hospitals, clinics, and various church functions where she was the main speaker. But many of these were never transcribed or translated. I got into contact with Joseph Kwakye, who, at the time, was a Twi language instructor for missionaries at the Divine Word Language School in Abetifi, and asked him for help. Two others from this school, Douglas Asomani and Kwame Fosu, also helped. Still others included Peter Kwasi Ameyaw, Vincent Adjepong, and Michael Owusu Nimako. Joseph, together with Douglas and Kwame, worked on transcribing the recordings and providing a solid English translation for Ghanaian audiences. Joseph was a good choice to lead the work. He lived in Afua's village (Atuobikurom) for several years as a teacher and was able to work directly with her on the text. But there were a number of difficulties. With me in the north and Joseph far to the south, communicating, comparing notes, and doing the editing and correcting was a big problem. To make matters worse, there was no telephone or mail service, the roads were impassible in the rainy season, the national bus service was down, and for much of the time there was no fuel for vehicles.

Because of these difficulties, I also tried my hand at the transcription and translation. Later, mine was compared with Joseph's. I was able to add a little to his text, but the main benefit of my efforts was that I got to know how much Joseph struggled. Transcribing the cassettes required the patience of a modern Job. Those machine-gun-like, staccato verses eluded the most attentive ear. One had to listen intently, over and over again. There were many words and phrases, hero allusions, and denizens of the unseen world that were archaic and unfamiliar. The West African dust and humidity have a disastrous effect on tapes, so the recordings themselves were unclear in spots.

With Joseph's completed transcription and translation in hand, there was still much to contend with. The oppressive "hot season" in the north could be almost unbearable. Temperatures ranged between forty-four degrees Celsius in the day and a relatively cool forty degrees at night. From January to May, the hot, humid air intensified and pressure-cooked everything, leading up to that wonderful explosion of thunder, wind, and horizontal rain that announced the "rainy season." I have not-so-fond memories of checking through Joseph's transcription and translation and paging through my dusty, dog-eared Christaller Twi dictionary, leaving muddy prints with my sweaty fingers. In the next moment, these same wet fingers were slipping off the keys of my typewriter as rivulets of sweat rolled down my face and dropped onto the dusty pages that I was typing.

Joseph's translation was solid but fairly literal. I wondered how to expand on it and do justice to all that was going on in Afua's praises. How would I explain or elaborate on the depth of meaning behind each phrase she used? How could mere words carry the enormous power of her allusions to folk heroes, chiefs, and their exploits? How could the rhythms, intonations, and melodies of her praises be rendered to convey all the beauty that was there? English is a combination of Greek, Latin, and Anglo-Saxon, with bits of Hindi and Malay-Bahasa, and even a tad of Inuit. It has more words and realms of meaning than any other language on earth. Yet there were connotations and meanings in Afua Kuma's Twi that simply did not exist in English. The task was daunting. I was reminded of the Akan proverb "A crab can't possibly give birth to a bird!"

A full rendering would require acres of footnotes and a long glossary. I had to ask myself how this could be handled in a way that would avoid stymieing the Ghanaian readers on the one hand, and that would increase their fascination on the other. In the end, I decided to stick to the basics. It was more important just to get the main corpus into the hands of the Ghanaian public and leave the finer points for later.

There were also difficulties in "just getting it into their hands." The late 1970s and early 1980s were a "hunger time" in Ghana. The rains had failed for several years in a row and, due to predatory leadership, the economy had failed. Most businesses were either closed or working at half their former output. After many attempts with various publishing houses—including the Catholic Press, which was run by my own missionary congregation—finally, in 1980, Peter Barker, who was then the director of Asempa Publishers of the Christian Council of Ghana, accepted it for publication. Peter immediately saw the great importance of the material, and he did everything he possibly could to promote it and guide it through the publishing process. There were many delays. The press had difficulty obtaining even such basics as paper and ink, and half the workers had been laid off. Without Peter's drive and continuous efforts, it would never have been published. But miracles do happen, and with hard work and great diligence, the problems began to recede, and the first copies of both the Twi *Kwaibirentuw Ase Yesu* and the English *Jesus of the Deep Forest: The Prayers and Praises of Afua Kuma* rolled off the press in 1981.

The above background to *Jesus of the Deep Forest* serves as a kind of *preface* to this preface. Now I would like to speak about the preparation of *The Surprising African Jesus: The Lost Prayers and Praises of Afua Kuma*. Over the past forty-plus years, the fame of Afua Kuma has been slowly spreading from Ghana to other parts of Africa and the Global North. In 2017, Angus Crichton, an editor for the Society for Promoting Christian Knowledge (SPCK) in the UK, contacted me about doing a new version for both Africa and the wider English-speaking world. Afua had gone to Jesus in 1987, but she still had something to say. We had not used all the material from the original tapes recorded in 1976 and, although I had often thought about publishing these, with all my moving about, I had never gotten around to it. My own set of tapes had long since disappeared. Spurred on by Angus, I began to ask around. As luck would have it, some were finally discovered in an old "chop box" of a friend from the Ghana days. It is from these squeaky old cassette tapes that this second outpouring of Afua Kuma's prayers and praises has been produced.

When this new project started, I had not spoken Twi for a decade, so I distrusted my ability to transcribe and translate the new text. Once again, the task of transcribing the tapes and making a good literal translation went to Joseph Kwakye. I was able to track him down and contact him in the Kwahu area, where he is now retired, and I sent him the tapes. As with *Jesus of the Deep Forest*, he was assisted by Douglas Asomani and Kwame Fosu. But now the cassette tapes were much older, and Afua Kuma was no longer there to help them. So, this time the work was a lot more difficult, and it took a longer time to complete. But, as they say in Ghana, "Slowly, slowly the chicken sips the water." A year and a half later, the chicken finished sipping, and I started work on his translation.

Progress was slow and sporadic. I had just started a new job which was completely different from anything I had done before, so I was faced with a steep learning curve. To slow things down even more, my religious superior had put me in charge of buying an older house in San Diego, fixing its many problems, furnishing it, and adding on two extra rooms. In short, converting it into a suitable "mission house," and all of this on a limited budget. These things took their toll on the project.

In this set of praises, Afua Kuma speaks to the Global North. This change of audience would require some extra work. I could not expect my readers from the Global North to have very much knowledge of African history, cultures, mentalities, or languages, so there would have to be many footnotes and a glossary. But descriptions and long explanations are still not enough to convey the "feel" of the praises or the very different world in which Afua lived. Many photos would be needed to help readers see Afua's world as she saw it. This time around, I also felt it was time to add to the "feel" of the praises through artistic expression and creative license. I wanted to give this new work some of the rhythmic flow and staccato beat of the original Twi. After trying several different modes, I finally settled on using iambic tetrameter, or poetic verse consisting of four metrical feet each consisting of an unstressed syllable followed by a stressed one. I have used this form throughout the piece. The versification adds to the poetic beauty and offers a truer sound to her praises, but it comes at the cost of sometimes having to stray from a more colorful literal meaning. It slights some of the Twi expressions, which were more prominent in *Jesus of the Deep Forest*. It also loses some of the stimulating impact of Ghanaian English, such as word order and the idiomatic expressions that Ghanaians love but which those in the Global North might simply regard as "bad English." Nevertheless, I believe that there is still enough local color to pique a curious Northern religious imagination and enthrall an avid Southern following who would like to hear more from their acclaimed spiritual mentor.

Acknowledgements

I JOIN THE WHOLE CONTINENT of Africa in giving thanks to "Afua Kuma, Yaa Asantewaa," the spiritual warrior whose faithful response to the promptings of the Holy Spirit has helped give the peoples of this continent the freedom to express themselves to God in their own way. It is a way that has its roots deep in their history. It has long been nurtured in their traditions and has been faithfully carried through the ages by the ancestors. But now it has exploded into a new and glorious form: giving praise to the Lord. The rest of the world also gives thanks to Afua Kuma because that once "dark" continent has now, through her praises, become a continent of Christian light. And it has not stopped there, for now every culture, every ethnicity, and every people throughout the world has been given a spectacular cue to begin praising Jesus in their own true, God-given way—and he is anxious to hear it.

Very special thanks must go to Joseph Kwakye, who labored over the squeaky old Twi tapes to produce the excellent transcription and translation which I elaborated on and versified. I also want to thank Douglas Asomani and Kwame Fosu, who were his stalwart helpers. Without Joseph and his deep knowledge of the Twi language and culture, without his persistence, patience, and eagerness to help, neither this work nor the original, *Jesus of the Deep Forest*, would have seen the light of day.

Special thanks must go out to all of those involved in making the recordings that lifted this phenomenon up for all to see and hear. Without their efforts, neither the first publication of Afua's praises nor this second output, *The Surprising African Jesus*, would have been born or even conceived.

They say that "the anthill and *keja* tree do not thank each other for favors because they are completely dependent on each other." Nevertheless, I am especially grateful to my friend and colleague, Fr. Steve Bevans, SVD, who wrote the foreword and took time out of his busy schedule to help with some of the editing. I have been encouraged by his support and persuasive insistence that this project must go forward. Without this, it would still be gathering dust.

I also wish to thank Mark Shaw for his beautiful watercolor sketch of Afua Kuma, Rosemary (Ofei-Kumi) Keatley for photos of her wonderful paintings, and the dozens of SVDs, including Rex Vegbey, who contributed so many of the beautiful photos that help us see the world of Jesus through the eyes of Afua. Many others have contributed to this project, and here I would like to thank them all, especially those who have kept the fires burning so that little Afua's Jesus may continue to surprise us and captivate new generations of seekers in the Global North, Ghana, and beyond.

Introduction

THE SURPRISING AFRICAN JESUS is a contribution of the "first order" to African/Ghanaian theology. In other words, it is not a reflection on an African theologian but the actual work of a contextual theologian—the theology in process of a grassroots African theologian. To be sure, it is different. It is that of an oral theologian—a rural, illiterate Ghanaian woman—but a powerful contribution, and a great contribution. It is not academic. But it is deeply theological. Today, theologians talk a lot about how it is the people that have to do contextual theology, and that we theologians are their midwives. Here is a good example of that. I am only a midwife here. In this introduction, my work is done. A more theological commentary, in my view, would even eclipse the main point of the text, which is to bring Afua's words/poetry/theology to the general public. If there is any theological commentary to be done, it will be done by the reader.

Once the work of Afua Kuma has been brought to the eye of the general public—academic or otherwise—I fully expect there to be a collection of essays engaging her work. But for now, what is presented here is the basic, grassroots text. Here, I simply introduce the text and try to explain, describe, elaborate on, and illustrate the many elusive, extraordinary, and often arcane references that Afua makes in the text. I might add that because the book is meant for a readership in the Global North, the one hundred images are a very important part of this explanation and illustration.

This is not the first time that Afua Kuma's prayers and praises have been in print. The first set was published in Ghana under the title *Jesus of the Deep Forest* in 1981. Since then, it has sold out at least three times and has made its mark with both regular churchgoers and academia. It has inspired several theological master's theses, and it has received recognition in scholarly journals. It was published for a Ghanaian readership, and both the English and the Twi version, *Kwaebirentuw Ase Yesu*, have been extremely popular with ordinary Ghanaians. Professor Gillian Mary Bediako, the current deputy rector of Akrofi-Christaller Institute (ACI) and the widow of my late friend, the celebrated theologian, Kwame Bediako, told me, "*Jesus of the Deep Forest* has had a significant impact on our master's and doctoral curricula and is a key source on oral African theology. It is a text for all our students."[1]

Before presenting this new volume of Afua's praises, I would like to address the question of why the first was so popular—why it always sold out and was read by thousands of students and ordinary Ghanaians, why a prestigious Ghanaian theological institute like ACI should make it required reading, and why all the visitors, doctors, and nurses in that hospital ward where I first encountered Afua Kuma and her marvelous praises could find them so captivating. What did these prayers have in them that made them so attractive, and what made Afua so special? The answer, as we shall see, is simple: her prayers radiate a true African spirituality through an oral art form that enlivens a long-overlooked source: the unvarnished daily life of a culture, a people group. It uniquely joins the world we see and touch with the elusive, unseen world behind the veil, and it does this in the form of Christian prayer that is uniquely African.

Here before us, quite paradoxically, are praises to Jesus dressed in a traditional African art form—something that has rarely been associated with Christianity. Afua's praises draw inspiration from everyday African life—hunting and fishing, farming, preparing food and eating, visiting a chief, and going to a diviner, or *malam*—and they confirm these activities and the relationships involved as intimately connected (positively or negatively) to the glory of God.

Afua Kuma sang her praises for only one reason—to give praise and glory to Jesus Christ.[2] Her image of Jesus is quite different from the images Ghanaians might see in their European-style prayer books. She presents Jesus as the "Greatest Magician" and as a "Diviner," "Warlord," and "General." She sees him as a great "Sea Hawk" who provides his people with fish, and as a fountain that nurses his children in water. Her Jesus is actively involved in their daily life. The devil also features prominently in their life. She depicts Satan and his followers as roasting like plantain on a charcoal fire.

Contextualizing, or grounding the gospel in important traditional beliefs, imagery, and holy places has been an integral part of the Spirit's mission since Jesus' incarnation and Saint Paul's discourse on "the unknown god" of the Greeks (Acts 17:23 ESV). Gradually, Roman pagan temples

---

1. Gillian Mary Bediako, email message to author, February 8, 2021.

2. Afua almost always speaks of Jesus (*Yesu*) but rarely of Christ (*Kristo*), which is difficult for Ghanaians to pronounce.

became cathedrals, the great halls of kings became basilicas, and statues of Hermes became Good Shepherds. In our time, these religious cultural contextualizations have begun to embrace all the world's seven thousand cultural traditions, ethnicities, and languages, including those of Africa. Early twentieth-century contextualizations in Africa emerged with the likes of Simon Kimbangu and the Prophet Harris. Their ministries brought to an alien Christianity a sense of familiarity and to African traditions a great expansion. To the people, they brought an aha moment—the kind that suddenly recognizes the new thing as always having been there. Suddenly, the old is clarified, expanded, and greatly enhanced.

One such contextualized occurrence was initiated in the late 1960s by Father Peter Kwasi Sarpong. Before he became archbishop of Kumasi, he was appointed as the cathedral administrator. Perhaps it was the combination of the Holy Spirit and his Oxford degree in anthropology that prompted the inspiration to arrange a special "Asante-ized" Corpus Christi procession down the main streets of Kumasi. Taking advantage of his kinship link with the *Asantehene* (chief of the Asante[3]), he commandeered the chief's own kente-cloth-draped[4] palanquin,[5] along with his horn blowers, drummers, and palace warriors with their "Dane guns" and monkey-skin helmets—the whole courtly panoply signaling the arrival of the king. When the surprised people heard the shooting of muskets, the droning elephant-tusk horns, and the booming *oba-barima* drums[6] announcing their unexpected king, they threw open their shutters and tumbled out into the streets to welcome him. Some were waving white handkerchiefs in praise, while others just

3. The Asante are the most prominent of the Akan, or Twi-speaking peoples of Ghana. In precolonial times, they controlled most of what is now Ghana, as well as parts of Ivory Coast and Togo.

4. Kente cloth is a costly and prestigious fabric that is woven in four-inch by ten-foot strips and sewn together to make a cloth that is worn on festive occasions. Traditionally, silk cloth brought from the Orient by Portuguese and Dutch trading vessels was unraveled and rewoven on narrow four-inch looms. The different patterns (*adwene*) each have names (e.g., "*Fatiah fata Nkrumah*"—Fatiah [President Kwame Nkrumah's Egyptian wife] adorns Nkrumah), and some can only be worn by high-ranking chiefs.

5. Great chiefs were carried by porters in a conveyance called a "palanquin," a term borrowed from Hindi.

6. Two important drums found in every chief's court include the *oba*, which means "woman" and refers to the smaller drum, and the *barima*, which means "man" and refers to the larger drum. The *oba* produces a higher tone and *barima* a lower tone. When they are used together in various sequences, they can mimic the tones of proverbs that are used to convey set messages like the death or arrival of a chief. They carry over great distances, leading to the name "talking drums."

stood there in awe. There in the palanquin, where they expected to see their king, was the Corpus Christi monstrance. This aha moment presented the church as already theirs, deeply embedded in their traditions. This was an entirely new picture of the Catholic Church, which had been a latecomer[7] to the Asante, and it opened the floodgates for conversion.

The same combination of astonishment and recognition was present when Ghanaian Christians heard Afua using the imagery and courtly language of royals at church celebrations in praise of Jesus. This was the kind of language that one would only hear from royals in chiefly courts. Now, it was used to praise Jesus! Afua Kuma's praises made Jesus familiar and intimately accessible. They connected Jesus Christ to everyday life—to their traditions, their art, and their religious imagination. This was not only surprising, it was audacious. The one offering these praises was a woman, not a man! This had never happened before. People would look up in amazement and ask, "Who is this who speaks like this? Where did she get all of this?"

In giving answer to these questions, I would like to borrow fairly extensively from the research done by Sara Fretheim.[8] While studying the life and legacy of Afua Kuma as an oral theologian, Fretheim was told by members of her family that Afua had royal blood. Although she was not raised in a chief's court, she seemed to be well versed in courtly language and customs. She was holy and had the spirit of a warrior. Fretheim maintains that it is possibly this royal connection, combined with her fame as a holy person—even a "holy warrior"—that invested her with the nickname "Yaa Asantewaa."[9] She was also a woman of great wisdom. Afua's grandson, Tetteh, explained to Fretheim that they called her "Afua Kuma, Yaa Asantewaa" because of the wisdom she displayed in settling disputes. People sought her out for counseling, prayer, and healing. Birth attendants went to her for training. The local chief asked for her help in deciding court cases, and the local Catholic priest asked her for help with his counseling cases.

---

7. The Reverend Fritz Ramseyer (1840–1914), a minister of the Presbyterian Church, was the first missionary to bring Christianity to the Akan. He first settled on the Kwahu Plateau and then proceeded westward to Kumasi.

8. Fretheim, "Jesus! Say It Once." I know of no other research that has been done on the life of Afua Kuma. The present work has been published more than a year after Fretheim's article, so some of Afua Kuma's words and phrases in this volume have been revised, edited, or changed and thus may be slightly different from those quoted in "Jesus! Say It Once."

9. Yaa Asantewaa (1840–1921) was the queen mother of Ejisu, who in 1900 led the Asante in an uprising against the British and was later exiled with other Asante royalty to Seychelles.

Fretheim points out that the term "warrior" fit her well considering all her ordeals and suffering. She was accused of witchcraft, and in vigilant prayer she fought for her son's freedom.[10]

Fretheim informs us that Archbishop Sarpong characterized Afua's praises as "deep words"[11] and "big words."[12] He said that the difference between Afua's praises and the forms used by chiefs is her central focus, which is on Jesus and "the Christian mystery." He said that some of her expressions are her own and proceed from her deep faith. However, the symbols she uses are traditional, even though many would not be used in everyday religious activities.[13]

Afua's royal bloodline certainly gave her the opportunity to hear, understand, and speak the special poetic praise language of chiefs (*amoma*) and that of the royal family (*adehyekasa*).[14] Her skill in using chiefly language could be compared to that of an *okyeame*, or royal spokesperson, who not only interprets for chiefs but diplomatically rephrases ordinary language in ways that uplift and verbally massage the listener. But the way Afua used chiefly language was broader than this. Instead of the regular chiefly use of alliteration, contrasting metaphors, praise appellations, proverbs, parables, and allusions to great heroes and chiefs, she connected these with Christian themes which made frequent use of biblical figures and scenes. She also employed a wide variety of other usages. These include a courteous or polite style of speaking (*obokasa* or *opokasa*)[15] and the speech style of elders (*mpanyin kasa*)[16] or "deep speech" (*kasa a emu do*), which is considered the language that every cultured or educated speaker of Twi should understand and use. And, of course, she also used the special speech style of women (*mmeakasa*).[17]

---

10. Fretheim, "Jesus! Say It Once," 35.

11. Fretheim, "Jesus! Say It Once," 27.

12. Fretheim, "Jesus! Say It Once," 29.

13. Fretheim, "Jesus! Say It Once," 29.

14. Characterized by a deliberate stutter and slight nasality.

15. Distinguished by the tone of voice, words of courtesy, and the use of *sebe* (meaning "excuse what I will say") before a statement that might be considered offensive or in bad taste.

16. It consists of the use of proverbs and parables (*mmebusem*), honorific praises (*mmeran*), praise titles (*abodin*), and metaphors of all sorts. It is the language that is used at public ceremonies and religious assemblies such as funerals, outdoorings of babies, installation ceremonies, durbars, and when making sacrifices or pouring libations.

17. Characterized by a lack of economy in the use of words and exclamations of

When all of these are put together, Afua's use of language is much broader than what one might hear from a chief or his *okyeame*. The clipped rhythm of her phrasing, her voice modulation, and her exclamations of joy, disgust, and bewilderment blend chiefly language with everyday speech, especially the speech of women. Into this mix she adds references to all of the different activities of ordinary Ghanaian life. But what distinguishes her praises more than anything else is that she uses them to praise the name of Jesus—not human kings, but our divine King.

Her praises are a tribute to the empowerment of women. The main style used by Afua Kuma in her praises is *mpanyin kasa*, the style used by the elders. This, in itself, is quite extraordinary. It is taken for granted that women understand and can use the speech style of elders, but they are not expected to use it publicly at special gatherings or occasions. Nor are they required to compete with each other, as men do, or prove how "cultured" or "educated" they are by how eloquently they speak. Their speech style is unmarked and taken for granted. It is expected to be spontaneous and unrestrained in contrast to men's well-regulated and controlled speech. Afua's hearers would not expect this "elder style" of speech from a woman. In Ghanaian society, gender roles are strong and not easily challenged. This would certainly add to their astonishment.

Some of the unusual elements of the "elder style" in Afua Kuma's praises include different names, focus markers, repetition, and contrastive metaphors for praising Jesus (e.g., "Mighty Tree," "Elephant Hunter," "Greatest of Rivers," "Living River," "Hurricane Wind," "Mighty Rock," "Giant Needle," "Butcher with Muscles").

Her use of focus markers gives us more information about Jesus (e.g., "Jesus, you are the Precious Kente"; "You are Lord of Travelers!"; "You are Women's Jewels").

Her use of repetition involves a variation of constants and contrasts in linguistic form, the repetition of single sounds, same syllables, same words, and same word groups, an identical beginning in one or more places, and the repetition of a word at the beginning, the end, or the middle of successive lines. These include:

a. Repetition of single sounds in close succession or at distant points (e.g., "shattered into a thousand blackened shards").

---

disgust, bewilderment, or alarm, e.g., *"Hweoo!"* ("Look at that!"), *"Eye nwonwa!"* ("It is amazing!"), *"Twea!"* (an expression for contempt).

b. Repetition of the same syllable in different words (e.g., "At some point in life, we were lost. At that dreadful time, we were tossed" or "Young warriors rise up before him. They come to praise and adore him").

c. Repetition of words and word groups (e.g., "to come for their meat and be filled—the meat of the young wild bull!" or "I listened to all that they said. All that they said wounded my ears").

d. Identical beginnings of one or more words (e.g., "yet all our enemies are dead! . . . yet all our enemies are dead!").

e. Identical endings (e.g., "All the youth assemble before you" and "your priests assemble before you").

f. Repetition of a word or phrase at the beginning, middle, or end of two successive linear units (e.g., "The mighty *osisiriw* tree has fallen on weak *onwama*. They will both soon fall to the ground!").

Besides the many bynames and praise appellations and the use of parallelism, we find many contrastive metaphors in her praises. These produce an unexpected outcome that reflects the wonderfulness, power, wisdom, goodness, or kindness of Jesus (e.g., "He is the Strongest of Fetishes"; "He plants his farm in the river"; "He farms his fish in the river"). Whether from the viewpoint of traditional Ghanaian culture or that of Christianity (e.g., "Jesus, our Savior in the past, receive our thankful praise today"), there is an element of contrast or reversal present either in the encoding of the words or in the accepted outcome. In this second English offering of her praises, in order to bring out the full impact of the spoken Twi, I have tried to incorporate the above devices wherever possible.

When Afua used these styles of speaking in her prayers and praises, it had an enormously powerful effect on her Ghanaian listeners. Professor Kofi Asare Opoku, an expert on the Twi language and culture, told Fretheim that Ghanaians have a special adulation for those who speak the language well.[18] He said that they were always surprised when Afua used these elements of style.

When Christian themes and imagery (e.g., Daniel in the lions' den or Naaman, the leper) were added to Afua's many references to nature, heroes, the king's court, and everyday objects and activities, the combination was astonishing and extremely moving. Sometimes it was even unsettling. As

18. Fretheim, "Jesus! Say It Once," 28.

mentioned above, in the Akan culture,[19] public speaking is reserved for men. To hear a woman use these styles in public was surprising and a bit shocking. Yet, when people heard her praises, they would be swept up by the sounds and images into a worshipful aura that captured their traditional religious imagination. In traditional Ghanaian thought, there is no division between the sacred and profane. By embedding Jesus into every aspect of Ghanaian life, Afua dissolved the inherent division that had been molded into the Christianity that was brought by the European colonial churches. Suddenly, there was a new way of being Christian that simply "felt right" to the people. It did not fight with their culture. It enabled everything in their lives to glorify God. Is it any wonder that Afua left her listeners spellbound?

She used her range of styles skillfully, even effortlessly. Professor Opoku told Fretheim that "her abilities were incredible," and that "she produced these praises effortlessly!" He said that she knew the language well, that her images were "just stunning," and that "a torrent of beautiful language" flowed from her mouth. It would only be normal for people to be surprised and ask, "Where did you learn how to do this?" Opoku told Fretheim that Afua's traditional response to this would be, "I was born with it, yɛde woo me." He said that when he heard her perform, it was very clear to him that it was a gift from God, for these things originate in the spirit world.[20]

Fretheim relates that Archbishop Sarpong concurs with Opoku—that Afua simply had a great "gift." He said that in oral tradition, the power of gifts cannot be underestimated. All around us, we see great people arising from humble origins. He said that people do have special gifts, and it is quite possible for someone from the bush to have such a wonderful ability.[21] When I first heard her proclaim her praises in that hospital ward, it was also clear to me that she truly had a remarkable gift.

Afua's style, imagery, and ability with language are all important elements of her praises, but even more important is the source, Afua Kuma herself. Her humility, compassion, generosity, deep faith and trust in God, and personal relationship with Jesus are the source and inspiration of her praises. The fact that she was a royal did not make her vain or feel that she was privileged. She did not look down on others or attribute any special

---

19. The overarching culture group encompassing the Asante, Fante, Kwahu, Akuapem, Brong, and many other subgroups.

20. Fretheim, "Jesus! Say It Once," 29.

21. Fretheim, "Jesus! Say It Once," 28.

importance to herself. She was never haughty or aloof but rather the opposite—quite humble and unassuming.

She was also uncompromisingly honest. Fretheim relates a story that Afua's grandson Tetteh told her that bears this out. In the story, Tetteh found a large amount of money and brought it to Afua for safekeeping. Later on, when he went to get the money, she avoided him. Eventually, he found out that she had gone around the village looking for the owner. When she found him, she returned the money. As a result, Tetteh became angry and demanded that Afua sell a sheep and give him the money. Afua was happy to do this for him.[22]

The people Fretheim interviewed also spoke about Afua's generosity.[23] They told her how Afua would take her grandchildren and some village children to the farm with her. At the end of the day, she would give them the largest portion of the harvested food but would never accept any money for it. Nor would she accept any money from the churches where she performed. Rather, the opposite—she often added her own money to the church offering. This was her way of helping the poor in the community.[24] They said that the churches always wanted her to proclaim her prayers and praises at their celebrations because it encouraged the people to give more generously. They said she only accepted a few small things like the occasional scarf or necklace.[25]

Beyond all her godly virtues—in fact, their very source and the criterion by which every aspect of her character should be judged—was her relationship with Jesus. A priest who knew her well testified that he had never seen anyone who had such a love for Jesus as Afua did.

Afua's prayers and praises paint a new and vibrant portrait of the Jesus we pray to—one that is filled with incredible imagery and color. For African Christians, they offer new ways to call upon Jesus. Her praises are reminiscent of the Psalms, but they add something more. They are Christianity in a new vein—in a way that has not had a chance to be heard before. They arise from the very heart of Africa and express what comes naturally to a people whose religious instincts are solid and profound. They leap up free from the entanglements of a "Western Church."[26] The words and phrases

---

22. Fretheim, "Jesus! Say It Once," 33.

23. Fretheim, "Jesus! Say It Once," 34.

24. Fretheim, "Jesus! Say It Once," 33.

25. Fretheim, "Jesus! Say It Once," 34.

26. The great twentieth-century theologian Karl Rahner refers to the culturological

are rooted in a rich African oral history. For centuries, they have been heard in royal halls giving praise and honor to chiefs and courtiers. Such contexts and events were always as much religious to the African mind as they were secular. But up until now, they have almost never been heard in the form of Christian prayer to Jesus. Unfortunately, these traditions have been overshadowed and constrained by Western Christianity. We need to take a moment to reflect on why this is so and why this special form of prayer had to wait for Afua.

Christianity and Western civilization came to Africa as a single package with one dominant message: everything African is bad and everything European is good. Christianity rode in on the wings of a colonial project where African worlds needed to be replaced; not encouraged. In Christian terms, African traditions and practices were not godly enough, or worse: were considered "pagan" and even "devilish."

When I first arrived as a new missionary in Ghana, I asked for a time to learn the language. Initially, my superiors did not see the need for it, but finally gave in. After a period of immersion learning, I took a test which was very short because my examiner quickly realized that I spoke better Twi than he did after his twenty-five years there. Then he said to me, "Okay, but you are not to use it—especially not in your sermons." I replied that this was the very reason I had learned it. Then he said, "We are not here to learn their language or learn about their things; we are here to teach them ours so that they may become good Christians." I do not say this to detract in any way from the missionaries of that era or their dedicated ministry to the people whom they dearly loved. But I want to emphasize the culturally one-directional approach to ministry that existed fifty years ago.

In African mission circles, church and chiefdom have long been "water and oil." From a Western perspective, the chief sits on his throne. But Ghanaians see the "royal stool" of their chiefdom as the place where the spirits of their ancestors convene. As such, it is not only royal but sacred—a kind of tabernacle. It was, and is, a chief's uncontestable source of authority and power. The fabled Golden Stool of Asante was more an altar than a throne. As such, it was venerated and regularly sacrificed to. In the past, Asante sacrifices sometimes required the lives of servants, slaves, and even other courtiers. I was given the Ghanaian name "Kwasi Antwi." Kwasi means "Sunday born," and Antwi, I was later informed, was the name of

---

transition which the church is undergoing from a "Mediterranean Church" to a "World Church" (Rahner, "Fundamental Theological Interpretation").

a famous Asante general who offered himself as the sacrifice that would ensure their victory over the British. Since I was a missionary, the irony behind the honor of being named after him was not lost.

Sacrificing to shrines inhabited by spiritual entities, which missionaries and colonial authorities have mistakenly termed "animism," did not strike missionaries as a suitable stem on which to graft the Christian faith. Nor were the social and political traditions and practices considered fitting foundations on which to build an "advanced" civilization. Many chiefs and most family heads have become Christian over time, but in doing so they have usually been forced to lead double religious lives—a personal "European life" in church and a communal "Ghanaian life" in their traditional religious obligations to their community or family. Although nominally Christian, their links with the African spirit world have first place.

In this atmosphere of wholesale rejection of all that is African, Afua's praises could not have happened. The yearning was there, but it was throttled. The African response to this was *anibue* ("Get your eyes opened to the modern world").[27] Ghanaians wanted to be like Europeans and enjoy their benefits—both spiritual and temporal. Few were privileged enough to join the British establishment, but anyone who wanted could join the "white man's religion" and gain "white man's knowledge" through "mission schools." In 1976, the catechist at my "bush" mission station in Chereponi had just returned from his training in the distant town of Wa. We organized a welcome-home party for him. During the celebration, his father came to me saying, "I'm so happy, I'm just sooo happy!" When I asked him why, he said, "Because my son has become a white man!"

Because of a thorough disregard for everything African, the hymnals that ended up gracing African church pews were those taken from the European canon—e.g., the *Westminster Hymnal* and the *Catholic Hymnal*. But Afua always sensed that there was something lacking in them. These hymns did not excite the deep religious feelings she yearned for. In Africa, religion and one's connection with the spirit world are not separate from life, as they so often are in the Global North. In Afua's world, courtly life in all its grandeur is both emotionally and spiritually uplifting. Why should Christianity be different? She yearned for all the goodness of her culture to be joined to the goodness of God. Shouldn't they all be one? God made

27. The phrase "Get your eyes opened" (*anibue*) refers to the entire Western colonial impact on Africa, which includes Christianity together with the secular European trappings—the power, wealth, and material prosperity of the "white man" (*oburoni koko*—literally, "red man from the horizon").

them, didn't he? This is what she felt. But she did not find the Jesus she yearned for in these hymns.

She realized that something was seriously missing, but she did not know what it was. It was vague, as if seen "through a glass darkly,"[28] and without any sharp focus. It was a deep, embryonic sense of longing that did not yet have a concrete object, so it remained silent and unexpressed. Without consciously realizing it or permitting herself to accept it, she yearned for the *oba-barima* drums of the chief's court, his gold ornaments and symbols, the beautiful colors and patterns of his kente cloth, and his enormous, flowing umbrellas. She felt that all the glory of the king's court—its goodness, beauty, and grandeur—should be recognized as true reflections of God. She wanted all of this to praise the name of Jesus. She wondered how such important parts of her life could be kept separate from her faith?

This powerful yearning continued until a breakthrough occurred which allowed the mixture of the water and oil. All of Africa—indeed, all peoples of the world—have had the same yearning to free their religious imagination and to praise the Lord using their own words and symbols. When the Bible was first translated into Twi, the people felt some measure of fulfillment. They said, "Now we see that the God of the Europeans is our God, too. He speaks our language; he is one of us." And what a difference that makes! If God loves us as we are, we are free to love ourselves—to be ourselves! It was as if God was saying, "It's okay, you can be yourself! That's the way I want you to be!" But God speaking to us in our own words is only part of the relationship. What about the other part—our response, our speaking to God? The demand for reciprocity compels us. God has spoken to us; now we need to respond. Here, too, we need to be ourselves.

A truly African Christianity was simply unthinkable until very recently. How could Afua or anyone know that there could be another way to be Christian, or what it would look like, or how it would sound? It was something that could only come from the Spirit when the time was right. When it came, it emerged in combination with a new civil identity, and it came in stages. Fighting alongside their colonial sovereigns in the two world wars helped to make Africans more conscious of their own unique and honorable identity vis-à-vis the rest of the world. This led to the movements for African independence in the 1950s and 1960s. Over the same period, beginning with Vatican II, the Catholic Church slowly began to "open its windows" to the world. These events made it possible for new

28. 1 Cor 13:12.

civil and religious identities to emerge together. Bibles were translated, and indigenous languages began to be used in the liturgies. By the mid-1970s, African symbols, artwork, vestments, hymns, and musical instruments began to replace the European hand-me-downs. This *sankofa* ("Go back to the origins and get it.") awareness was also fostered throughout the 1960s and 1970s by the US civil rights movement. Blacks began to show pride in their origins and wanted to be called "African Americans." People in Ghana also started to take more pride in their origins, and the unnamed yearning started to take concrete forms.

There are various accounts of how it took concrete form in the words of Afua Kuma. My own recollection involves a special dream that brought everything to a climax. I do not remember where I got the information about her dream—whether from Afua or from someone else. None of my informants could verify it. But somehow, I came to understand that one night during a distressing time in her life, she dreamed that an angel or messenger of God came to her and told her not to be afraid to pray using the words that rose from her heart. She began praying them in the dream and awoke with these powerful words of praise pouring from her lips.

Fretheim's account of the origin, which was obtained from Afua's family members, does not mention a dream but rather that it was a gradual development. She was sick and depressed, and, at first, she prayed privately in this special way. Then, she gradually gained more confidence and started to pray publicly. Afua's grandsons, Tetteh and Ofori, said that this happened between 1969 and 1979. Another origin account was given by Afua's daughter, Beatrice Fantoaa. She said that Afua started praying in this way after hearing a moving sermon about giving thanks in all circumstances. At the end of the sermon, the preacher invited everyone to pray. Then Afua amazed those present with praises that no one had ever heard before. Beatrice said that from that time onward, her mother prayed with the "new tongue" that God had given her to praise Jesus.[29]

Whether Afua's breakthrough came in the form of a dream angel who assured her and gave her "permission" to speak from her heart, was inspired by a sermon, was a slow process of confidence building, or came from all these together, the result is the same. She began to pray in this way publicly. When she saw that people liked it and were moved by it, she gained confidence and gradually lost any feelings of shyness or guilt. She was finally free to use the imagery that inspired her and the rhythms and cadences

29. Fretheim, "Jesus! Say It Once," 26.

that surrounded her and lifted her spirits. Having gained this confidence and freedom, she realized that she must use the proverbial expressions of her people and the praise songs that echoed from the chief's palace. She felt impelled to include all the normal, everyday things that made up her life—the majestic trees of the forest and the myriad creatures that populate it, the sights and sounds of the home, the farm, and all the good things of her world. She finally realized that all these wonderful things must be returned to their source and give fitting praise to God, the Greatest of Chiefs, who dearly loves his creation. This was something new and wonderful. It was truly Christian, but no longer European.

All of this could not have happened if Afua was not a woman of deep faith. Like most villagers, she managed a small farm, but she was also a respected traditional birth attendant (TBA), or midwife. Fretheim tells us that in 1961, Afua started learning to be a TBA by working with other TBAs. Later, she received training from the Catholic Sisters at Mary Queen of Peace Church. Her deep faith was shown in her work as a TBA. Fretheim relates how Afua's daughter-in-law Jane, also a TBA, described what Afua would do when she reached the house of a patient. First, she would wash her hands and then pray that God would protect the mother and child. Then, she would ask the Lord to guide her hands so that she wouldn't make a mistake. Finally, she would ask the Lord to bring the whole process to a successful conclusion. She would begin her work with the mother only after she finished praying. Fretheim gives us this prayer that Afua Kuma prayed: "When you heed the things of God, you need not wear an amulet to make your marriage fruitful. A woman is struggling with a difficult labor, and suddenly all is well. The child, placenta and all, come forth without an operation. He is the Great Doctor!"[30]

Her deep faith produced a spirituality that was clearly expressed in her praises and in her gift of spiritual healing. Afua's family told Fretheim a story about this, which I summarize as follows: A certain woman brought her daughter, whose name was Rebekah, to Afua for prayer. The girl had already died, but the woman kept trying to revive her. First, she took her to the fetish priests. But they declared her dead and said that they were not able to help. Then, in a state of desperation, she went to Afua. So Afua gathered some members of the house together, and they prayed for the child. All of a sudden, they heard a loud noise. When they went outside to look, they discovered that Afua's big sheep had fallen over dead. This happened

30. Fretheim, "Jesus! Say It Once," 30. For Afua's prayer, see Kirby, *Deep Forest*, 14.

at the same moment that the little girl "was resurrected," and for this reason they call the girl "Resurrected Rebekah."[31]

Drawing on information from Afua's family, Fretheim says that Afua was brought up in the Presbyterian Church and that she attended the Catholic Church for some time. But she joined the Church of Pentecost (CoP) as an adult. She mostly identified as a member of the CoP because of her daughter Elizabeth's marriage to Pastor Nartey, and because she felt that the CoP was "growing in glory." Fretheim relates that Afua's family said she admired the CoP because she felt it was a very "modern institution." She admired their European-style clothing and their use of English instead of Twi.[32] Fretheim also comments on how Afua's son-in-law would often take her to proclaim her praises at church events. Her grandsons said that she was always ready to go when it came to doing the work of the Lord, and that she would immediately put aside whatever she was doing and go with you.[33]

Because Afua's religiosity was deeply rooted in her culture, it easily attracted Akan people from all the different Christian denominations. Catholics appreciated her and considered her to be Catholic. Pentecostals considered her Pentecostal. In his interview with Fretheim, Father Henry Kwaku Duah said that Afua promoted ecumenism, especially in the way she brought people together. Afua wanted to help people, regardless of their religious affiliation. Father Henry said that she helped to bring greater unity between Roman Catholics and other denominations. There was a true spirit of ecumenism that cut across church lines whenever she prayed. Fretheim notes that several women whom Afua met at the Catholic mission in Kwahu-Tafo said that they were so impressed with Afua's praises at various Catholic celebrations that they started to offer similar praises, and that Afua encouraged them and gave them some training.[34]

Such a gifted spiritual healer and praise singer was bound to experience challenges from the dark side. Before Afua started to proclaim her prayers and praises publicly, she suffered intensely and went through a true "dark night of the soul." In particular, she suffered from the false accusations and death threats of a fetish priest who was the custodian of a witch-catching

---

31. Fretheim, "Jesus! Say It Once," 31.

32. Like other Ghanaians, Afua liked the good things that Europe and modernity brought, and clearly experienced an inner conflict between these and her deep Ghanaian identity.

33. Fretheim, "Jesus! Say It Once," 25.

34. Fretheim, "Jesus! Say It Once," 26.

Tigare shrine.[35] According to Fretheim, there were illnesses and deaths in the family, all within a short period of time. The Tigare priest accused her of the witchcraft that had presumably caused these misfortunes. He tried to force her to prove her innocence by going through the shrine's ordeal, which involved eating a poisoned kola nut. She regarded this and other forms of spiritual oppression as manifestations of Satan and his devils.[36] Her resistance against these forces comes out strongly in her praises.

The great power of speaking out the name of Jesus is related to this, and is a theme that comes up frequently in her prayers. Fretheim relates how Afua's uncle encouraged her to keep repeating the name of Jesus as a defense against the oppressive powers of the fetish priest. He believed that this would expose the real culprit. So, Afua went around saying, "Jesus, Jesus, Jesus."[37] Then, one night a strange woman came by and heard her saying the name of Jesus. According to the story, she immediately left the scene, and from that moment on the children's health improved. As a result, the people came to believe that this woman was responsible for the misfortunes and not Afua Kuma.[38]

Besides repeating the name of Jesus, Afua persisted in her prayers for deliverance and vindication. Fretheim relates the following: "The fetish priest lost patience and came and said he would kill her within seven days if she did not face the ordeal. Afua Kuma boldly said that seven days was too short a time for him to prepare and said he should . . . take forty days." Then, she warned him that if she lived, everyone would know that she was innocent and that he did not have the power to kill her. But if she died, then he should take a piece of her clothing as proof that he had killed her.[39]

Fretheim goes on to say that during these forty days, Afua prayed in private. When they ended, it was clear that the powers of the fetish priest were no match for the powers of God. Fretheim relates that Afua joyfully declared, "Jesus will come when you call; from very far he hears you!" and

---

35. An "earth shrine," originally from Tano in northern Ghana, that was brought to Asante in the 1920s in response to a rash of witchcraft accusations that occurred in that period. It spawned a witch-catching cult that spread rapidly throughout Ghana and became popular again in the 1950s during the unsettled period before independence.

36. Fretheim, "Jesus! Say It Once," 31.

37. Fretheim, "Jesus! Say It Once," 31.

38. Fretheim, "Jesus! Say It Once," 32.

39. Fretheim, "Jesus! Say It Once." 32.

"Jesus! You say it once and the matter is settled; in all the world, you have the final say!" After this, she continued to pray in public.[40]

Sometime later, Afua met the fetish priest while traveling by train to Cape Coast. She said to him, "I'm sick just now but if I die, it's not you who did it, you couldn't kill me!" Fretheim says that "he was embarrassed and tried to give her some money to cover over his offence." But she refused it and told him, "If your ways are perfect, the Lord will make your way straight and make your enemies flee before you!"[41]

The fetish priest was greedy. Afua's family explained to Fretheim that her brothers had been quite wealthy and that Afua Kuma would inherit some of the money. Therefore, the priest proclaimed that witchcraft was in their house and that he would remove it if they gave him all their gold and valuable cloth. But Afua held to her faith in Christ and boldly defied him.[42]

At this time, Afua was also grieving over her son. Fretheim explains that during the presidency of Kwame Nkrumah (1957–66), her third-born son, Joseph Ofori, worked as a driver for the minister of education. A bomb blew up the minister's car, and Joseph was arrested. But Afua believed that God would deliver him, and with prayer and fasting, she "fought" for his deliverance. Eventually, he was able to flee to the USSR.[43]

Given Afua's liberal use of Akan traditions in her praises, it may seem surprising that she suspected many aspects of Akan culture. Her experience of being accused of witchcraft and an earlier traumatic experience set her against most of the traditional Akan religious activities. Fretheim relates that Afua "took a very firm stand against traditional religious practices and would not let her grandchildren . . . attend cultural dances because she felt that they were associated with 'fetish.'"[44] Afua felt that Jesus was the only true answer to their traditional problems. She said, "Our ancestors didn't know of *Onyankopon*: the great God. They rather served lesser gods and spirits, and became tired. But as for us, we have seen holy men, and prophets. We have gone to tell the angels how Jehovah helped us come this far; with great gratitude we come before Jesus, the one who gives us everlasting life."[45]

---

40. Fretheim, "Jesus! Say It Once," 32.

41. Fretheim, "Jesus! Say It Once," 32.

42. Fretheim, "Jesus! Say It Once," 33.

43. Fretheim, "Jesus! Say It Once," 24.

44. Fretheim, "Jesus! Say It Once," 34.

45. Fretheim, "Jesus! Say It Once," 35. For Afua's prayer, see Kirby, *Deep Forest*, 30.

Although Afua saw some aspects of her traditions as harmful, she recognized others as particularly good and godly. The CoP offered her greater freedom to express a spirituality that was firmly rooted in these more wholesome and holy aspects of daily life. She felt that the strong personal relationship she had with Jesus would help her to discern the difference and carry on his work. Fretheim remarks that after her husband's death, Afua remained unmarried. Over the next twenty-five years of her life, she chose to do God's work. It was during this time that she trained as a TBA and began to travel around to Christian celebrations and events offering her praises.[46]

There is a time and place for everything, and I believe that the arrival of Afua's praises on the African scene was a Pentecost event—one of the times that the Spirit is manifested. The Akan believe that a person can encounter spiritual realities in dreams and that these have the power to change one's life. When Afua sat up in bed praising the Lord, or when, after a long process, she began to praise Jesus in her own special way, it was the Spirit who was speaking. Suddenly, her words were authorized by the greatest King of all. Now, it was not only permissible but absolutely necessary for Afua to proclaim them. This has prepared the way for others to follow her lead. When Ghanaians hear her praises, they understand that God has validated a side of their life that has long been suppressed, hidden, and almost forgotten. Now, it is not only permissible to give full expression to one's culturally embedded spirituality; it is not only right and true, good, and beautiful; it is also necessary. Afua opened the way for African life in the Spirit.

In his interview with Fretheim, Father Henry talked about the limitations of that period—the 1960s and early 1970s—and how incredible it was to hear the praises of Afua Kuma. He reminds us that there were no drums in Catholic churches, and he even told of a man who was so shocked when he first heard drums in church that "he almost died of an asthma attack." Father Henry recognized that "Afua was ahead of her time culturally."[47]

At that time, several friends and I were trying to promote Asare Bediako's wonderful, Scripture-based Twi hymns that were accompanied by drums and guitars. Although Bediako was a Catholic, the church would not accept them. But they were welcomed in the CoP and independent churches. One of the most beautiful hymns was "*Gye me tata.*" When a

46. Fretheim, "Jesus! Say It Once," 25.

47. Fretheim, "Jesus! Say It Once," 26.

Ghanaian mother is teaching her child to walk, she kneels before the child with open, outstretched arms, beckoning to the child and saying, "*tata, tata*" (an untranslatable bit of Twi onomatopoeia). The hymn calls on our Mother God to "give us *tata tata*."

God has used Afua Kuma to unwrap the cocoon of Western cultural forms that have swaddled the infant African Christianity. Her prayers and praises have cut through all the theological and liturgical differences of the many European-modeled Christian denominations that have sought to make African converts in their own image. The prayer and praise forms that she uses pierce though all of this and go to the heart of the matter— Africans connecting with God as persons formed in God's own image. It is an image that African ancestors have formed through the ages as they connected with their Grandfather God (*Nana Nyankopon*) in all that he has created.[48]

Afua's prayers and praises serve as an impassioned call to peoples everywhere, and not just Africa. They are a call to trust the holiness of our deep cultural foundations. This deeper message behind Afua's praises is both simple and true—that God is, indeed, present in a special way in every one of the world's cultures. That God wants all of them to be recognized, and that he longs to hear all our voices praise and glorify him, each in our own special way. It is all part of his glorious plan—that we are created to praise him in the highest and most beautiful ways that our cultures have prepared us to praise him. And thus it is meant to be, for his is the kingdom, and the power, and the glory forevermore. God chose Afua Kuma to let this message resound throughout the world.

48. In Akan culture, grandfathers are expected to be loving and generous. Fathers are disciplinarians.

Images

1. Weaving a strip of kente on a traditional loom (3).[1]

2. They were waving white handkerchiefs in praise (3).

1. Throughout this section, the numbers in parentheses identify the page on which each phrase appears. Phrases in quotation marks are directly quoted from Afua Kuma's prayers. Phrases without quotation marks reference material from the introduction.

3. They beat their *oba-barima* drums (3).

4. "Jesus, Bright Star of the Morning" (71).

5. "Jesus, . . . your priests assemble before you" (71).

6. "The priests are . . . performing on stringed instruments" (75).

7. "Sun and . . . rain make use of their powers in vain" (72).

8. "Jesus, the Elephant Hunter" (72).

9. "Growing his yams in . . . the surging waters of *Senkyi*!" (72).

10. "They carry great headloads of food" (72).

11. "Let us . . . joyfully don our kente" (73).

12. "It is Jesus who sees all things" (74).

13. "Our God-man is not to be feared" (76).

14. "[Let them] bear him high on palanquins" (77).

15. "For now I am human again" (77).

16. "He, the Strongest of Fetishes" (78).

17. "The things I have done weighed on me" (78).

18. "He . . . [will] buy us a two-story house" (78).

19. "Jesus farms his fish in the stream" (78).

20. "Great chiefs are going before him" (79).

21. "The devil staggers on the path" (80).

22. "The thick *Sakyi* fog surrounds us" (80).

23. "He . . . cares for his band of children" (81).

24. "His is the food that satisfies" (81).

25. "This heavenly bread is from God" (81).

26. "Jesus' bullets kill elephants!" (82).

27. "We have taken our holy baths" (83).

28. "Others are waving their banners" (83).

29. "Jesus stretched out his hand for us" (83).

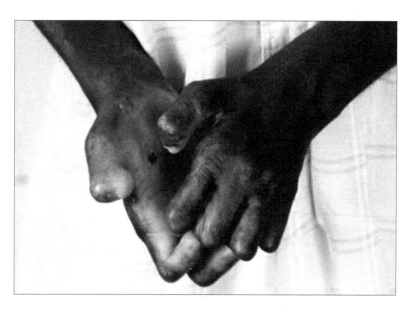

30. "Come and see the lepers made clean" (86).

31. "They run far off to . . . where elephant grass is blazing" (86).

32. "Put me into a lions' den" (87).

33. "I choose my words from the Bible" (88).

34. "Now I proclaim the word of God" (89).

35. "Precious gifts for our young Savior" (90).

36. "We bowed before him in worship" (90).

37. "He calls you to come from the mud" (91).

38. "Drummers, bring your assorted drums" (92).

39. "Drums, let us hear your pounding beat!" (92).

40. "Receive our thankful praise" (92).

41. "Let northerners . . . beat their flexible drums" (93).

42. "See the multitude of people from all the nations" (93).

43. "We fall on our knees before you" (93).

44. "Your daughter is here . . . praising your name" (93).

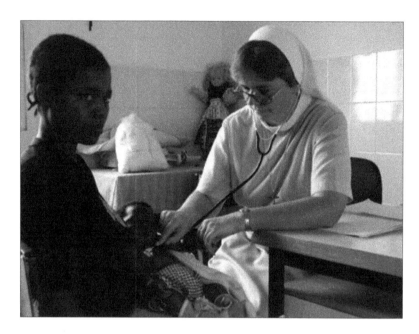

45. "Does the fetish priest have a cure?" (96).

46. "But now his cross is our compass" (97).

47. "Should I praise him with instruments . . . ?" (97).

48. "I will follow the priests, who take the lead in processions" (97).

49. "It made my face shine like the moon" (98).

50. "He fixed the sun in position" (98).

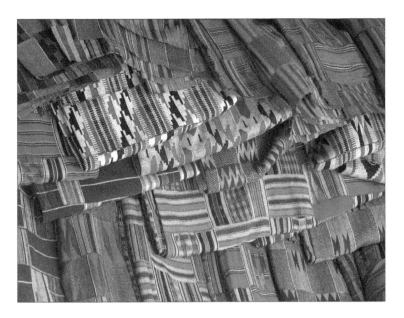

51. "You are the precious Kente Cloth" (98).

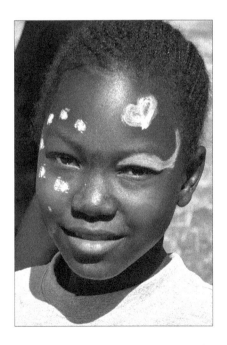

52. "You brighten our celebrations" (98).

53. "You are the . . . Silk Scarf, which we use to cover our heads" (98).

54. "You are the Violent River" (99).

55. "You are the Treasures of Women" (99).

56. "You nurse your creatures in water" (99).

57. "He was standing there on the sea performing . . . wonders" (100).

58. "His wind was dragging fishing nets" (100).

59. "Fishing nets . . . spanned the sea from east to west" (100).

60. "All the new converts are dancing" (101).

61. "When the pastors turn to face them" (102).

62. "You will burn like a piece of roasted plantain" (102).

63. "Those he has bathed and anointed" (105).

64. "They appear like the rising sun" (105).

65. "Their kingly robes color the sky" (106).

66. "They fall . . . prostrate before him" (106).

67. "They carry babies at their backs!" (108).

68. "He hunts the biggest of the lot" (108).

69. "He is going to hunt big game for widows" (109).

70. "He is the Keen-Eyed Sharpshooter" (109).

71. "The moon defends us from behind" (112).

72. "If you go to drink of this Font, everlasting life will be yours" (112).

73. "The pastors . . . will wash you and anoint you" (112).

74. "The heavy *kontonkurowi* covers them like a canopy" (115).

75. "We traveled that fearful road" (115).

76. "A lion was there to greet them" (115).

77. "A green mamba was there to meet them" (115).

78. "I dreamt of bulls—brutal bush cows—following me" (116).

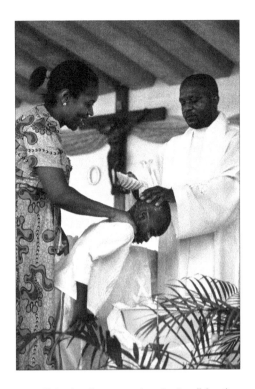

79. "The day the pastors baptized me" (116).

80. "Bush cows have vanished from my dreams" (116).

81. "Jesus, you are the Mighty Tree" (116).

82. "Jesus, you are the Mighty Rock" (117).

83. "With a thorny crown I greet you" (117).

84. "The Humble Lamb I lead to death" (117).

85. "His death cross gave us his Spirit" (117).

86. "Before you reach that inner door" (117).

87. "Your waters supply us with fish" (117).

88. "Jesus, you are the Deep Forest" (118).

89. "You are the Greatest of Rivers" (118).

90. "You feed us hunks of hippo" (118).

91. "Of fishermen kin, I have none" (118).

92. "We harvest elephants, huge hippos, and fat wild boar" (118).

93. "Jesus, the Sea Hawk, hooks our fish" (119).

94. "So bright the light in Jesus' house" (119).

95. "Let him merely extend his hand" (119).

96. "Like dancing kings at a durbar" (120).

97. "You will see them shining like stars" (120).

98. "Jesus' touch is like a cannon" (120).

99. "His blowtorch hand . . . ignites a raging fire" (120).

The Surprising African Jesus

Jesus, Bright Star[1] of the Morning,
    All the youth[2] assemble before you.
They come to be dressed in kente.
    Oh Jesus, the Greatest of Kings,
your priests assemble before you.
    They are playing their instruments,[3]
while the young men prime their muskets.
    They shoot volleys in your honor.

Jesus has gathered his people
    to put on a grand performance.[4]
He, who is the Richest of Kings,
    has offered us a golden bird[5]
to entertain the gathering.
    A gold umbrella[6] shields us.

1. Stars feature importantly in Akan cosmology. Early morning is the time to discuss important things, such as resolving a dispute or repairing a damaged friendship.

2. The Akan, like all African peoples, organize themselves by age groupings: "children" are from about three to twelve years, and the "youth" are from twelve to around forty for men and from twelve to eighteen for women. At this stage, the men are warriors, and both men and women are workers. Next is the "domestic group," when the women marry at eighteen, raise children, and take on the household duties, while the men (ages forty to sixty) become married fathers and providers. The modern need for education has changed this. Now, women marry later and men earlier. The final stage is that of the "elders." For women, it begins after menopause, when they are often referred to as *obabarima* ("woman man"). They are the leaders of the women, have greater freedom, and assume greater responsibility in society. They also exercise considerable influence over men, including the male elders. Men become elders and exercise civil and religious authority over the community around the age of sixty.

3. The Akan, or mainly Twi-speaking peoples, use many different kinds of musical instruments and drums on different occasions and for different purposes.

4. The reference is to festive meetings of dignitaries in which subchiefs honor the king, or paramount chief.

5. "Golden bird" refers to an insignia of the Asante king.

6. Akan chiefs go in procession in the towns and villages under huge, elaborately

The scorching sun and beating rain
    make use of their powers in vain.
He invites us to sit with him
    under his golden umbrella.

Jesus, the Elephant Hunter,[7]
    killed three[8] of these ponderous beasts.
He does not permit his helpers
    to bring us our portions[9] of meat.
He carries them to us himself.
    He presents them to our widows[10]
while his high priests sit and observe.[11]
    What is left, he gives to orphans.

Jesus, the Unmovable One,
    he plants his farm in the river.
See him at work in the water,
    growing his yams in the river—
the surging waters of *Senkyi!*[12]

Jesus has come from the river.
    His priests have come along with him.
They carry great headloads of food—
    a bountiful feast for widows.

---

decorated umbrellas, which are more for sumptuary display than for shade.

7. Hunters are considered special in Akan lore—especially elephant hunters. They are protected with special amulets and spiritual powers to be able to go up against dangerous animals. These protections also apply to warriors, or "hunters of men." The vengeful spirits of the men and animals they have killed may come to them in their dreams.

8. Gifts are given in threes so as not to appear inhospitable or stingy, which is a great offense. When things are done in threes, it means they should never stop. This is sometimes signified by the saying *"Odo nsa da"* ("Love never ends").

9. When a slain animal is divided up, the portions are given out according to a specified regimen. Chiefs get one of the hind legs; the hunter gets the other. The women and children receive the back and the trunk.

10. Here is a nod to Scripture. Widows should receive charity because they have no one to care for them. This also applies to Ghanaian villages, where they become a burden and are often the victims of witchcraft accusations.

11. A reference to Jesus acting as a servant, e.g., washing the feet of his disciples.

12. *Senkyi* refers to the swift-flowing part of the Volta river by the Akosombo bridge.

Children are crying this morning.

 Yet, widows, do not be afraid!

Jesus has hitched up his horses

 and mounted his *katapillas*[13]

to carry home plenty for all.

 You, widows, do not be disturbed!

Bring your empty stomachs to him

 and let them be filled with his fare.

He tells his children not to cry;

 to come for their meat and be filled—

the meat of the young wild bull![14]

 So let us gather together,

and joyfully don our kente—

 a royal garb fit for a feast.[15]

Many were climbing to Jesus.

 Their climbing to him has been blocked.

The devil has put them in chains!

 So, Jesus has sent forth his priests

with the keys to unlock their chains.

If you should eat their tabooed[16] meat,

 Jesus is able to see it.

Jesus, the Greatest Magician,[17]

---

13. From Caterpillar Inc., a company that produces large industrial machinery like bulldozers, backhoes, and trucks. In Ghana, it refers to a bulldozer or any large piece of earth-moving equipment.

14. The "bush cow," or Cape buffalo, is the most dangerous of all the wild animal kingdom. To receive a portion of this animal from a hunter is a great honor.

15. A reference to the parable about the king who prepared a wedding feast for his son (Matt 22:1–14): "He asked, 'How did you get in here without wedding clothes, friend?' The man was speechless." (Matt 22:12).

16. Among the Akan, many foods are forbidden because of certain conditions, such as pregnancy, undergoing a special ritual or medical treatment by a "medicine man" (*adurufo*) or herbalist (*dunsinni*), or when under the curse of an ancestor. Such prohibitions are more to avoid the potential ritual pollution than from fear of becoming sick.

17. "Medicine men" and earth-shrine custodians (*abosomfo*) usually rely on their special connections with various spiritual entities or on the spiritual properties found in the herbs they use, or in a combination of these, to heal the infirm and perform "magic." All such wonders are believed to have a spiritual source, just as all illnesses and

can see us wherever we go
and knows everything that we do.
>Jesus is the Gigantic Tree.
When you perch upon its branches,
>you see all that there is to see.
It is Jesus who sees all things—
>both inside and outside his house.

He is truly *Tutu ampa*.[18]
>Truly, he is the Greatest One.
He strolls through the smoke of battle.
>His right hand holds ammunition[19]—
gunpowder, missiles, and bullets.
>Jesus is the Violent Wind
that defends his worried army.
>Jesus himself is their Armor.[20]
He stands there in front of big guns.
>His left hand catches cannon balls.
His right hand is holding a sword
>that chops his enemy to shreds.

He has made his priests the victors!
>Jesus helps those who offer help.
Those who give themselves to others

---

misfortunes are believed to have an otherworldly final cause.

18. "Truly the greatest one."

19. The Akan and other peoples of West Africa have used flintlock rifles, or "Dane guns," for war and hunting from the mid-eighteenth century up to the present time. Lead balls for ammunition were extremely hard to obtain, and hunters often substituted round stones or pieces of metal. Supplies of flints were also at a premium because they were carefully controlled by the British. The best flints were mined from quarries near Brandon north of Bury St Edmunds in England.

20. The idea of sacrifice for protection is a dominant theme in African religion. This has led to an extremely popular printed picture of the face of Jesus topped by a cruel crown of thorns and covered with blood and gore. The inscription under it reads: "I am covered with the blood of Jesus." It can be found in the homes of Ghanaians of every tribe and Christian denomination, for it commemorates Jesus' act of sacrificing himself to save us. It testifies to the fact that the prominent traditional religious theme of sacrifice has jumped over to Christianity, giving this picture, and those like it, the function of a powerful Christian amulet against spiritual attack.

get all the help they need from him.
The priests are coming to Jesus
　　　performing on stringed instruments.
Young warriors rise up before him.
　　　They come to praise and adore him.

You cannot escape from Jesus.
　　　If you attempt to run from him,
you are running away in vain.
　　　He will not attempt to follow
but will be with you just the same.

Sakyi[21] is the thick, misty fog
　　　that is not afraid of people.
We are encompassed by this cloud.
　　　But you, oh Lord, are not afraid
to lead your army through the mist.
　　　Your hurricane winds crush cities!

He is *Kwaforoamotakyi,*[22]
　　　the Laughing Chimpanzee.
If he should meet our enemies,
　　　he slays them with his smiling face.
That is what laughing Jesus does!

If you are not ready to fight
　　　but insist on going to war,
there is nothing that you can do.
　　　You will quickly scurry away
on small, retreating, crab-like feet
　　　that are shaky and unprepared.

---

21. People, animals, and natural monuments often have bynames or nicknames. Often, saying the real name is too dangerous. Here is one for a deep fog that covers the forested lowlands in November.

22. The chimpanzee. Chimpanzees have the personal byname, "Takyi," i.e., "Takyi the Chimp."

The hypocrite, *ananwonam*,[23]
> has approached to tell us some lies.

Let us go and tell the Strong Man.
> He is *Okuruakwaban*,[24]

the Stoutest of All Stalwart Men,
> and startled liars run from him.

Jesus listens with patient ears.
> He judges not us but our deeds.

Go and tell him all of your cares.
> Some are afraid and run from him.

But he tells us never to fear.
> Our God-man is not to be feared.

I have entered the battlefield—
> into the hands of my rival.

I, who have deserted my own,
> and have ventured far from my home—

I stubbornly sit on the chair,
> which says to all, "I do not care."

I may have been a fetish[25] priest,
> a soothsayer,[26] or a *malam*[27]—

23. One who pretends to know everything but doesn't.

24. An extremely strong person.

25. "Fetish" is a generic name applied to all the traditional amulets, shrines, and holy places associated with the elaborate Akan spirit world. The Akan distinguish between the different services and functions of the spirits, as well as their powers and limitations. They also distinguish between different shrine custodians and religious officials. The English term "fetish priest" could be used for any of these—the head of a household (*abusua panin*) who sacrifices to his clan's ancestral spirits, a diviner (*okomfo*), the custodian of an "earth shrine" (*obosomfo*), or the shrine of a bush spirit. It could also refer to the "owner" of a witch-catching shrine, a "medicine man" (*adurufo*), a herbalist (*dunsinni*), or a *malam*.

26. Soothsayers, or diviners, serve the public not by seeing the future but by "seeing" into the "unseen world" to determine the spiritual cause behind a client's misfortune. He prescribes what needs to be done to correct the problem. This usually involves a sacrifice to placate a disturbed spirit.

27. A *malam* is a Muslim marabout, or wandering cleric. They often act as diviners and "medicine men" by first discovering the spiritual source of a problem or misfortune and then providing a solution by appeasing the spirit that is involved through prayers or offerings to a higher power, God. They also offer various "medicines" in the form of

who will kill for you if you ask—
>   or armed robber by the roadside
awaiting someone to rob.

But now, oh life-giving Jesus,
>   I am only here to praise you.
Come and receive my thankful praise!
>   Let strong men from the northern plains[28]
come and beat their drums for Jesus.
>   Let the "macho men"[29] bring litters
to bear him high on palanquins.
>   For now I am human again—
no longer am I a robber.

All the goods that I have taken,
>   I offered no payment for them.
I said, "I am going away;
>   I'll come again later to pay."
But now I am tangled in debts.
>   It is like hot, melted rubber[30]
has been plastered into my hair!
>   I attempt to pass by quickly
as I cast my eyes all around.
>   I fear that I might be noticed.
The things that I didn't hear well,
>   I gossiped about them and lied.

---

amulets or passages from the Qur'an sewn into small leather pouches. These are used to prevent misfortune and offer spiritual protection.

28. The West African savannahs are the grassy "orchard bush" that extend from east to west across the width of Africa between the forest to the south and the Sahel bordering on the Sahara to the north.

29. In recent years, many young men have taken up weight lifting and bodybuilding to offer their services to builders for heavy construction or to gangs of robbers for criminal activity.

30. Rubber plantations (introduced in 1898) are common in the rain-forest areas of the Akan people. The viscous white sap of the tree is boiled into a thick consistency. The picture presented here is this boiling-hot, thick substance covering one's body.

The things I have done weighed on me.
>I have borne them upon my chest.
But he has tied his cloth to mine
>and lifted the weight off my chest.
These things weighed heavily on me.
>I have carried them on my back.
But he has tied his cloth to mine
>and has taken them off my back.

He, the Strongest of Fetishes—
>we put our confidence in him
to buy us a two-story house.[31]
>Jesus is the Giant Needle
that cannot be found in a bag.
>It is hidden in the lining.
Jesus farms his fish in the stream
>where they multiply and grow fat.
The fattest of these he gives to us.
>Those huge herrings and fat catfish
are offered by River Afram.[32]

The *mmenta*[33] and the *nsanku*[34]
>are inviting us to listen.
We can hear the sound of angels.
>They are calling us to join them
with horns, and flutes, and violins.

We are hard and unresponsive.
>We think he can do us no harm.
The mighty *osisiriw*[35] tree

31. To own a multistory house was a prestigious sign of wealth and, formerly, the desire of every Ghanaian household head.

32. A river in the eastern Asante and Kwahu region flowing through the Afram plains into the Volta.

33. A type of stringed instrument.

34. A type of stringed instrument.

35. A large, majestic hardwood tree of Ghana.

has fallen on weak *onwama*.[36]
They will both soon fall to the ground!
Look at *fitikokonini*.[37]
Will you ask it for fine perfume?
It lives all its life in the dirt
and has never taken a bath!

Jesus is there in procession.[38]
Great chiefs are going before him.
How splendidly they escort him,
giving him honor and tribute!
It is not for us commoners—
we the ordinary people—
that they have arrayed themselves so,
but rather in praise of Jesus.
It is him they wish to honor.

You are a wandering *malam*,
weak and without any power.
Though the little that you have
is still enough to kill a man.

Jesus is the River Afram,
who puts food in empty stomachs.
The *Enwii*[39] and *Asubone*[40]
are your swiftly running servants.
Their churning rapids boil our food.

36. A tree of soft wood that is useless for building or making charcoal.

37. The "antlion." Scientific name: *myrmeleontidae*.

38. Important occasions, such as the funerals and other gatherings of important chiefs, are celebrated with parades involving the chiefs and their retinue, including their subchiefs, courtiers, litter carriers, drummers, and horn blowers, with warriors shooting their flintlocks, women fanning the chiefs, young men playing various stringed instruments, and dignitaries carrying the gold-plated symbols of the chiefs.

39. A river in Asante.

40. A river in Kwahu.

Jesus Christ is the Rustling Leaf
      that makes the forest bend and sway.[41]
He, the *Senkyi*, gives us the meat
      of hippo and tilapia.

A shrewd liar is the devil.
      He comes to tell God's people lies.
The devil bids you, "Be seated."
      He says that he will protect you,
and gives you black powder to drink.[42]
      He says when you go to your farm
and you meet a dangerous snake,
      "Do not be afraid or alarmed."
He says it can do you no harm.

The devil staggers on the path,
      lurches and leans from side to side,
and into a bottomless pit
      he falls—broken, silent, and cold.
Katapilla has crushed his head!

Whenever the priests move about,
      Jesus guards in front and behind.
The thick *Sakyi* fog surrounds us,
      but our gathering has no fear.
The Cyclone has swept it away.

You saved us from our enemies.
      The youth have been marked with your seal—
anointed, they belong to you.
      So, tell them not to be idle.
Tell them not to be shallow or vain,
      and from useless conduct refrain.

41. The once-great forests of southern Ghana extended from the coast three hundred miles north from the sea to the Kintampo escarpment and from the border with Cote d'Ivoire in the west to the border with Togo in the east. Now, sadly, there are only a few islands of primary forest left.

42. This can refer either to calcinated herbal medicine for healing illnesses or to the black magic powder used for protection or harm. Both are mixed with water and drunk.

Now they belong to Jesus Christ—
      and this they must never forget!
Let them bring your good news to all,
      that all may be caught in your net.

Go to him when you are jaded.
      He gives meaning to lives adrift.
Resentment turns to contentment;
      the return to laughter his gift.
He is the Excellent Father
      who cares for his band of children
and takes delight in their laughter.
      He sees us, then runs to his farm
to give us whatever we need.
      His is the food that satisfies.

Can you see him there at his farm
      in between the sun and the moon?
He uses clouds as stepping-stones
      to gather his mountain of food.
Then he instantly drags it home
      with his bulldozer and horses.
He farms his fish in the river,
      then serves our supper on the bank
and prepares our beds for the night.
      He is our Life-Giving River,
and in him we make our abode.

The food he prepares is splendid.
      Not one of us has seen such fare!
He serves us our marvelous feast
      from between the sun and the moon.
This heavenly bread is from God.
      It comes from the blood of Jesus—
this food of life that he gives us.

Let us give thanks to Jehovah
>and hear some of his new praises.
I went out to visit the camp,
>where the enemy pitched their tents,
and quickly returned to the youth—
>the armed young men[43] of Jesus' camp.
If we try to launch an attack,
>no chance would there be to succeed.
Who can withstand their massive might?
>Our guns have no ammunition.
We are weak and cannot resist.
>To go on will only mean death—
bad death[44] at the hands of our foe.
>To turn back is our only hope.
If bad winds should carry us there
>to the fearful edge of their camp,
only mournful sounds will be heard—
>pitiful voices calling for help.
Go and tell Jesus your troubles.
>Shout to him that we need his help!

Jesus' bullets[45] kill elephants!
>A wonderful thing has happened.
The priests who were leading our youth
>have all turned around and gone home.
They were not vanquished in defeat
>but returned to sing his praises
and offer their prayers to Jesus.
>His praises are the weapons used

43. The *aberantekuw*, or warrior age group (ages twelve to forty).

44. Unexpected deaths are anomalies. The people believe that they do not happen by themselves or by chance. Rather, they are caused by enemies through spiritual means, especially witchcraft. Related to this are the so-called "bad deaths," which include suicide, death alone in the bush, or any sudden death. Those who die in this way are not given a normal burial. Their body is discarded unceremoniously in the "bush," where the dangerous spirit of the deceased is imprisoned by powerful "horn medicines." They do not become ancestors, and their names are struck from group memory, never to be used again. The fear is that they will reenter the family line (be born again) only to taunt and disgrace the family by dying a "bad death" once again.

45. Large lead musket balls, or twelve-gauge shotgun slugs, that can kill elephants.

to overcome our enemies!

What kind of Muscle Man is this?
       You enter his army to fight.
You do not go forth to battle;
       yet all our enemies are dead!
What manner of Warlord is this?
       Not one foot stepped into battle;
yet all our enemies are dead!
       They brought us sickness and disease,[46]
pain and bad death to our children,
       sudden and cruel death to all.
They sought our injury and harm.
       Only destruction did they bring.
Yet, our enemies have fallen.
       They are lying dead at our feet!

Our enemies bring us troubles.
       But we have no need to fear them.
We have taken our holy baths.[47]
       Our bodies have been anointed.
We lie happily on our beds,
       watching Jesus crush our foe.

Do you hear his army singing?[48]
       His priests are singing songs of praise.
Some play musical instruments.
       Others are waving their banners
to celebrate our victory.
       Listen to the words of their song:
"Jesus stretched out his hand for us.

---

46. Some common diseases among the Akan include malaria, typhoid, epilepsy, jaundice, skin ulcers, tuberculosis, diabetes, "river blindness" (*onchocerciasis*), polio, hypertension, and bilharzia.

47. A reference to baptism. Ghanaians bathe at least twice daily. The evening bathing is accompanied by a rubdown with shea-nut oil. This is considered the quintessence of health and contentment.

48. Such honorifics are usually given to a chief, a hero, or a warrior after a great victory.

He aimed it at the enemy,
and they have been burnt to cinders."
That is how we sing and praise him!

One day we heard a frightful noise.
Our army ran over to see.
The devil stood there petrified,
just shouting and screaming in pain.
He heard that Jesus is coming—
then, terrified, he screams in pain.

By this we are taught a lesson:
the devil is a deceiver.
He comes only to tell us lies.
When Jesus comes, Satan weeps blood!
Whenever Jesus approaches,
the wards of the devil go there,
making the devil scream in pain.
When Jesus comes, the devil screams!
The devil and his followers
were cast into a blazing pit—
the blazing pit prepared for them.
Let all the nations shout, "Amen!"

Oh pastor, I come for your help.
I come to confess my troubles.
Give me a seat[49] and let me speak.
All through the night, I had no sleep.
I lay, eyes opened, on my bed.
Sleepless was I throughout the night.
Since daybreak, no food have I touched.
I heard the curses of my foes.
I listened to all that they said.
All that they said wounded my ears.
Deep in my heart, I am troubled.
Let us go tell the Great Warlord,

49. When entertaining a visitor, it is good etiquette to offer a seat, then water, and only then have the person state their mission.

the One Who is Strongest of All.
        Tell him to come to our defense;
to save us from all that we fear.

The pastors say they will not go!
        They will not tell the General.
The youth all say, "We will not go!
        We will not tell *Tutu-gya-gu*![50]
We will not inform the Warlord."
        Jesus, the Patient Listener—
we will not tell him our troubles!
        He is the Greatest General,
who is feared by every nation.
        Is there any need to tell him?"

He, the Knife That Cuts Through Iron—
        him, we will not run to inform.
He, the Mighty Man most feared—
        we will not let the slightest breeze
blow him a hint of our troubles.

When we went to Jerusalem,
        Jesus was not there with his priests.
He was already crucified.
        It was his name that rescued us.
So, try to be peaceful and calm.
        Allow your enemies to come.
If the priests merely say his name,[51]
        in that instant your foes are dead.
Jesus' name will shatter their ranks,
        will drive misfortunes from our midst,
and will cast them into the sea.

---

50. The great warlord.

51. Names bear the spiritual imprint of the ancestor whose name is bestowed on the infant at the naming ceremony. Knowledge of a name, therefore, gives power over the one named, for the spiritual source is known and can be controlled by sacrifices.

When priests said the name of Jesus,
>   the devil wandered aimlessly,
and, in the deep forest, was lost.
>   The priests merely whispered his name,
and the devil plummeted down!
>   He summersaulted seven[52] times,
and he lies there broken and bent.

When priests say the name of Jesus,
>   come and see the lepers[53] made clean,
the cripples[54] jumping and dancing,
>   and the barren[55] nursing their twins!

The priests say the name of Jesus,
>   and the deaf[56] are able to hear,
and the blind are able to see,
>   and the dumb are able to speak.
The name of Jesus does wonders!

When priests say the name of Jesus,
>   the devil and his minions burn.
They run far off to the grasslands,
>   where elephant grass is blazing.[57]
If you run there with the devil,
>   fiery walls will surround you.

---

52. This is one of the special numbers in Akan lore. It is connected to the seven days of the week and the seven "day gods." Afua links seven to Saint Peter's question about how many times one must one forgive one's enemies.

53. Leprosy was once a dreaded disease in Ghana, but now there are mostly "burnt-out" cases.

54. Polio has claimed, and still claims, many victims in Ghana.

55. The greatest curse on any woman or family is that of barrenness. Children are not only a blessing, they are also a guarantee for the future of the family and the main form of social security for the parents in their old age.

56. *Bobo* is a general term used for a deaf person among all the peoples of Ghana.

57. Each year in the dry season (November to May), the grassy plains of northern Ghana are burnt by hunters in their attempts to catch game. A change in wind direction can have terrible consequences.

The name of Jesus makes one brave!

The priests called the name of Jesus!
      Whenever they say Jesus' name,
I feel daring and courageous.
      "Crucify me;[58] I do not care!"
Jesus' name makes me strong and brave!
      "Put me into a lions' den;[59]
in Jesus' name I have no fear!"
      When the priests shouted Jesus' name,
we hurdled through thorny[60] brambles.
      We charged onto the battlefield
and took our enemies captive.

The name of Jesus brings me home!

I am a runaway child.
      I have turned my back to my home.[61]
There is no one who chases me,
      yet I am always on the run.
I wander aimlessly about
      with my face to the wild "bush"
and the back of my head to home.
      I flee a sparse and tranquil wood[62]

---

58. She is not afraid to show her faith or to carry her cross, as Christ did.

59. A reference to Daniel. The lion is still "the king of the jungle." Today, wild lions in Ghana are to be found only in the Mole National Park.

60. The wild parts of the savannahs are dotted with thornbushes. Some areas are so thickly covered with them that they are impenetrable, and weaker animals, and sometimes humans, can hide in them for protection.

61. In a traditional setting, the home, or "compound," is not only a physical structure, it is also the locus of one's primary identity, one's ancestral line, and the group/place where one ultimately belongs. The bodies of the ancestors are buried in the center of the compound. One must go through them to contact all the spiritual entities with whom the ancestors had communion. They are the powers that protect the household and its members wherever they go. It is the source of their life. The people take a piece of this earth with them when they relocate. In the past, one had to be buried in the compound to become an ancestor.

62. Newly planted, or "secondary," forests are quickly taking the place of the primary forests. Some giant trees from the primary forests are more than a hundred feet high,

toward one that is dense and fearful.
      Then priests spoke the name of Jesus.
They asked him to send stormy winds[63]
      that would toss me back to my home.
Now I have found my home in him.

The name of Jesus does wonders!

I used to move with armed robbers,[64]
      and I enjoyed their stolen goods.
The priests called the name of Jesus.
      Now I detest the robber's life.
I want nothing to do with them.
      Now I move only with Jesus.
The youth of Jesus are my friends.

The name of Jesus transforms me!

In the past, I was dishonest.
      I sidestepped those who challenged me.
I started arguments for fun
      and encouraged fights and quarrels.
The priests spoke the name of Jesus.
      Now I have left those hateful ways.
I choose my words from the Bible.[65]
      Those who care to listen to them
will hear Jesus' name and be saved.
      They will receive fullness of life—
eternal salvation is theirs.

---

with trunks that are eight to ten feet in diameter (e.g., the famous "Big Tree" near Akim Oda).

63. Powerful winds begin and end the "rainy season." Sometimes, these can reach one hundred miles an hour and can knock down trees and take the roofs off buildings.

64. This is a more recent phenomenon beginning in the mid-1980s. Robbers get weapons from the armed services, or they are manufactured locally in the massive *Konkrompe* junkyard of Kumasi.

65. Afua had a great love of the Bible, and she knew it well. She could recite "chapter and verse."

Jesus' name does wonderful deeds!

See the drunkards[66] and prostitutes;[67]
     see those who pillage and profane—
these were my only companions!
     Then priests called the name of Jesus.
Now I proclaim the word of God!
     All those who listen to his word
have abundant life with Jesus.

The name of Jesus does wonders!

In the past, I bore false witness.[68]
     I testified with lies in court
and was paid for my evil deeds.
     I gained from others' misfortune.
The priests called the name of Jesus,
     and the Holy Spirit drew near.
Now I bear witness to the truth.
     I proclaim the good news of God
to those who are poor and needy,
     and all who hunger for his word.
They come from the east and the west,
     and are led by a brilliant star[69]
that shines from the kingdom of God.
     We have all gone out to meet them.
They are wonderful to behold!

66. Indigenous alcoholic drinks like palm wine and *akpeteshi* (distilled spirits) in the south and *pito* (sorghum beer) in the north of Ghana are quite strong. Alcoholism is a serious problem.

67. After a few years of schooling in the villages, instead of marrying and settling down, many young women go to the cities seeking a better life. But living is expensive. When they cannot find jobs, they often take up part-time prostitution. They are disgraced, and their future is uncertain.

68. Western-style courts are often used by citizens simply to punish each other and make government officials like lawyers, judges, and the police rich in the process. One would often find more justice in the chief's court, but even this is changing due to the need for money.

69. The star that guided the Magi.

Let us listen to new praises!

We laid precious gifts at his feet—
     precious gifts for our young Savior.
We bowed before him in worship—
     bowed down without raising our heads.
My brothers, please let me tell you:
     the two of us were petrified.
Not an inch did we move our feet.
     Not a *pesewa*[70] did we give.
He did not take a single gift,
     yet gave himself as ransom.[71]

Why do you sit there in the dark?
     Later on, let it not be said
that you never heard his message.
     The pastors have been preaching it.
The evangelists proclaim it.
     If deafness prevents your hearing,
you will hear it on that last day—
     on that final day of judgment.[72]

Elders, do not poison the youth
     with useless thoughts and earthen gods.[73]

70. An out-of-use copper coin worth one cent, but the same size and shape as the British twopence.

71. The price of our salvation was the blood of Jesus. In the Ghanaian mentality, we are thereby indebted to him. This process of reciprocation is shown by a Ghanaian proverb: "When you eat your brother's chicken leg, yours is walking on one foot."

72. The scriptural reference to "that day" has a powerful effect on Ghanaians. The day of reckoning awaits us all. One can often see this printed on the back of trucks and other forms of public transport.

73. There are several grades of "gods" among the Akan. The creator God is at the top of the pyramid. Below him are the various spirits of the earth that relate to larger territories and bodies of water where a tribe may reside. Below this are the spirits of "the house," or the ancestors. Following this are the spirits of nature and "the wild," which have special powers that can be used by individuals or fetish priests to accomplish their aims. Below this are the personalized spirits, or guardian spirits, in charge of the welfare of each individual person. All of these, except the creator God, have their shrines and shrine custodians. Headmen, or paramount chiefs, are in charge of the territorial shrines (earth shrines). Family heads are in charge of household shrines, and individuals

Some are destined to be leaders
        They will give their lives to Jesus,
and be blessed with wisdom and truth.
        They will take care of their people,
and all will be saved on that day.
        Be careful not spoil the youth
with useless cares and man-made gods.
        Let them be strong and change their ways
so that all of you may be saved.

You who are lying in the mud,[74]
        Jesus is calling you, "Come out!"
He calls you to come from the mud—
        from that filthy mud and be saved.
Whether you are a fetish priest,
        a soothsayer, or a *malam,*
who uses charms and talismans[75]
        to kill the body and the soul,
or robbers on the forest path,
        or prostitutes in the cities,
no matter what you did before—
        no matter how evil your past—
Jesus Christ wants you to be saved.
        If you turn away from him now,
will you turn to him on that day?

---

sacrifice to their personal shrines. One day when I asked the elders why they were going up to the earth shrine with a chicken, they said: "We are going to put food into the mouth of trouble." The Akan have no shrine for God except *Nyame dua* ("God's tree"), which is is located in the middle of the compound and is for food offerings but not bloody sacrifice. This is because "God cannot be bribed!" The Akan also had the practice of throwing food offerings over the compound wall as an act of petition to God. But normally, they would go to a *malam* to intercede for them through prayers (*adua*); or they would give "white offerings," like food, to beggars; or put an egg, rice, or bits of white cotton string at a crossroads; or give an egg or uncooked grains of rice to children. The presence of Christianity has replaced the need to go to a *malam* for God's intervention, but people still go to diviners, and sacrifice remains the most important way to either prevent or resolve trouble.

74. Physical cleanliness is important to the Akan, who bathe two times a day.

75. Another word for an amulet.

Jesus said that when he is raised,
　　　he will draw all things to himself.
So, let us go to praise his name,
　　　before he is raised to heaven.
Drummers, bring your assorted drums;
　　　begin playing your *atumpan*.[76]
You know the praiseworthy titles
　　　that honor the name of Jesus.

You are the Wonderful Husband—
　　　Caretaker of your family.
Jesus, if you don't help us now,
　　　there is nowhere else we can go.
You who are always close at hand,
　　　if you do not come to our aid,
then we are lost—no one can help!

Jesus, our Savior in the past,
　　　receive our thankful praise today.
The instrument players have come.
　　　Let them start playing their music.
Let it praise and honor your name.
　　　Singers, give him your songs of praise.[77]
Drums, let us hear your pounding beat!
　　　Nnawuta and *aduwuro*,[78]
you instruments of King David,
　　　and you, the *mfirikyiwa*,[79]
all of you come and play the songs
　　　that praise and glorify Jesus.

---

76. A large drum played in pairs. The so-called "African talking drums" cannot be used like a telegraph to send ordinary messages. They can only convey well-known drumbeat messages like, "The chief is coming" or "A great man has died."

77. Praise songs are sung by specially trained courtiers and praise singers to honor chiefs, heroes, and great men and women, or people in the place of honor at durbars, solemn processions, state events, funerals, and other festivals.

78. These "gong-gongs" are used both as musical instruments and to announce something important to the village.

79. Another type of Akan musical instrument.

Let northerners play their *nnonno*.[80]
    Let them beat their flexible drums
as they lead him in procession.
    Let porters[81] put on their head pads
to carry him high on their heads.
    As the procession moves along,
priests are preparing their head pads
    to carry the Bible on high.
They carry the actual word
    that comes from the mouth of Jesus.

We have come to hear some stories.
    They are astonishing and true!
See the multitude of people
    from all the nations of the earth.
I include myself among them.
    The devil has hurled us all
into a great morass of mud.
    I am ashamed to be with them.
We are mired and cannot move.
    Our feet are bound with muddy chains.
Jesus made a rope of his blood
    to pull us out of the mire.
Thousands of tongues roar out his name,
    giving praise for what he has done.

We turn to him for what we need—
    and all that we need he gives us
with his generous, gift-giving hands.
    Jesus, Merciful and Mighty,
we fall on our knees before you.
    Great and Merciful Jehovah,
your daughter is here at your feet
    bowing low and praising your name.

---

80. An hourglass-shaped drum with cords attached to the skins and running down the sides, which can be squeezed to change the tone of the drum. It is used in northern Ghana.

81. Porters carry supplies, but in this case, they carry a great chief in his palanquin.

I know I am not sweet smelling
        because of the things I have done.
But I have put you in my heart
        and my body feels good again.
I feel like a human being.

My fighting and robbing are done.
        I am done with litigations,
with my witnessing to falsehoods,
        and my lies under oath in court.
My roaming with bad companions,
        my untrustworthy relations,
and all my evil deeds are done.

These things no longer pull me down.
        I now have Jesus in my heart.
The things I bought without paying—
        those things, I have paid for them all.
Now I pay for all that I buy.
        No more am I *ogyeakawe*[82]—
the one who never pays his debts.

It is all by the grace of God!

Sometimes when I sat in the hall[83]
        and I heard them coming to me—
people to whom I owed money—
        I would rush to my inner room
and listen to what they would say.
        But now when I sit in my room
and I hear their voices outside,

82. A strong term of abuse.

83. A traditional Akan "house" (compound) is a series of rooms laid out in the form of a square with a space in the center for domestic activities. There are individual units all around the perimeter and an entrance at one end facing the road or lane. Members of the extended family live in the individual units, which usually consist of a "chamber," or sleeping room, and a "hall," or meeting area. The square room was introduced to the Asante people in the eighteenth century by wandering Muslim clerics. Before this, round huts were used. They are still prevalent in northern Ghana.

I leave my room to welcome them
and give them whatever they need.

It is all by the grace of God—
      all by the power of his word.
Now when I buy it on credit,
      have no fear you will not collect.
Jesus will send it on the wind.
      You will receive it on the breeze.
All will be filled with his riches
      and end our need for borrowing.

Stormy clouds may thunder and clash,
      but have no fear of the lightning.[84]
All your unpaid debts have been paid.
      Our God of Thunder paid for them.
That thunderclap was his payment!
      The greatest of all has been paid—
the debt that was paid with his blood.

How did I come to owe so much?
      Why am I such a worthless thief?
When I made the devil my friend,
      he heaped his massive debt on me.
Woe to you if he is your friend.
      He will lay his debt on your head.
It is like hot glue in your hair
      that works its way down your body
and covers the cloth[85] that you wear
      until all are stuck together.
It wrestles you down in its grip
      and prevents you from getting up.
You are troubled and cannot sleep,

84. A reference to the so-called "rain medicine" which will strike the thief with light-ning if he does not bring back the things he stole.

85. Men wear one large, toga-like cloth over the left shoulder. Women wear two smaller cloths—one around the waist and the other over the left shoulder like the men. Children (and in former times, household slaves) wear one cloth tied at the back of the neck.

bound and constrained by iron bands.

When the devil levies his dues,
        they come as worries and troubles,
as illnesses and sudden death,
        hardship, poverty, and disgrace.
In desperation and despair,
        you behave like one who is mad.[86]
The things that you didn't hear well,
        you tell[87] everyone that you meet.
You tumble and turn in your sleep,
        tormented by unwanted thoughts.[88]
Agitation and restlessness
        are partners who offer no peace.

Does the fetish priest have a cure?
        He has no treatment that can heal.
His only medicine is death.
        Pitiful tears wash over me.
My only hope is in Jesus.
        A priest once told me, "Stop crying."
"Follow me to Jesus," he said.
        "Only when you belong to him
will tears stop washing over you."
        I followed him and met Jesus.
I saw the cross and was restored.
        Peace and joy are my companions.
My spirit is calm and peaceful.
        Those terrible specters are gone.

86. Mad people, or those suffering from mental illness, can be found in almost every town and village wandering aimlessly about. People freely give them food and sometimes clothing, but otherwise leave them alone. Children sometimes harass them with shouting and provocative ditties.

87. As in any tight-knit village community, gossip is a favorite pastime, especially among elderly women.

88. "Thinking" usually has the connotation of being worried or obsessed about a problem that is constantly on one's mind, as in the Ghanaian English phrase "He has lost his job and is thinking too much."

At some point in life, we were lost.
　　　At that dreadful time, we were tossed
like tiny leaves in a torrent—
　　　a time when life was abhorrent.
We were not aware of our plight,
　　　our faulty course, or where it led.
But now his cross is our compass.
　　　By dying, he showed us the way.
On this Rock our lives are anchored.
　　　Let us give our thanks to Jesus!

At first, I did not know the way,
　　　where to go, or what I should say.
Should I praise him with instruments
　　　or join the group of praise singers?
What must I do to praise Jesus?
　　　I said, "I will follow the priests,
who take the lead in processions,"
　　　and that is what I chose to do.
They are anointed and ordained.
　　　It is Jesus who ordained them.
They are filled with wisdom and truth.
　　　I have chosen to join the priests.[89]
Their words point the way to Jesus.

These words of life poured over me.
　　　They bathed and oiled my body.
Truthfully, for over a year
　　　no water has touched my body.
It was the glory of Jesus!
　　　He ordained and anointed[90] me!
Wherever I go, they ask me
　　　if I have washed, or had my bath,

89. Here, Afua Kuma refers to "prayer camps" and jamborees of the Pentecostals and other Christian groups. Afua Kuma was often invited to lead prayers at these assemblies.

90. This is a reference to the anointing, or dedication, of a person or an object chosen by God, e.g., the anointing of Aaron as high priest of the Israelites (Exod 30:30), of the sons of Aaron and the tabernacle (Lev 8:30), or of David as king of Israel by the prophet Samuel (1Sam 16:13).

or rubbed my body with oil.

  When I pass by another way,
they ask me the same thing again.

  Although, for more than four days now,
I have not even washed my face.

This oil that anointed me

  made me known and gave me honor.
It made my face[91] shine like the moon,

  and it gave me blameless children.
By God's grace, I have my children—

  only by the grace of Jesus.
They are the priests and the pastors.

  These are my exalted children.
By the grace of God, they are mine—

  these children who belong to God.

Let us praise the Lord Jehovah!

  He loves to do the things he does,
and he does all of them so well!

  He fixed the sun in position
and set the earth in its orbit.

  He is the God of our customs.
He is using our traditions

  to build a glorious mansion.

You are the precious Kente Cloth

  and the colorful Dutch Wax Prints.
You brighten our celebrations.

  We marvel at your majesty.
The fame of your splendor has spread.

  All the world has come to know you.
They all admire your beauty.

  You are the wonderful Silk Scarf,
which we use to cover our heads.

  You are the Unbreakable Stone,

91. Afua's understanding of her charisma is that she has been anointed or chosen by God.

which cannot be smote by a fist.
       You are the Violent River,
which one cannot blockade[92] with sand.
       You are the Powerful River,
which no bar of sand can oppose.

You are the Lord of Travelers!
       Your gospel reaches every land.
You are the Eagle at daybreak
       that carries us on our journey.
You are the Treasures of Women,
       their Veil and Beautiful Clothing,
their Fine Ornaments and Jewels.
       You are their Hearth and Cooking Pots—
you, the Gentleman of Judah!

How did you make such a river?
       It ebbs and flows without ceasing.
It constantly goes on its way
       without a beginning or end.
All have seen your wonderful deeds!
       You nurse your creatures in water.
How can they live beneath this flood?
       Are they able to dig a well?
How can they keep chickens or sheep?
       Within a day, all will be dead.
Jesus is their life-giving source.
       They thrive and grow in his water,
and they daily grow in number
       to give us food in abundance.
All are eating giant catfish![93]

Everywhere, people are running.
       They all want to stay with Jesus—
the one with everlasting life.

---

92. Jesus is an unstoppable force in our lives.

93. Catfish, especially the large variety called *odo*, are a favorite delicacy among the Akan.

When the people got to Jesus
and were standing at the seashore,
        the priests were gathered there with them,
baptizing them and praising God.
        Jesus was standing on the sea
beaming forth brilliant shafts of light—
        brighter than the sun and the moon.
So brilliant was his shining light
        that the sun became dark as night.

He was standing there on the sea
        performing marvelous wonders—
playing musical instruments,
        which were hanging on a rainbow.[94]

His wind was dragging fishing nets
        that spanned the sea from east to west,
to draw the multitude to him.
        His *nyanno*[95] drummers were with him
keeping the tempo on their drums.
        Thunder and lightning are the drums
that are played by *nyanno* drummers!

You pastors and priests, have you heard?
        Those you baptized are calling you.
They want to come and see Jesus,
        but the sun is stabbing their eyes.
Tell them: "Dance to the instruments
        that resound from those brilliant gates.
For none can behold his glory
        with eyes that are merely human."

Let them dance to the lofty sounds

94. The rainbow is associated with the presence of God. The most important word
for God in Akan is *Nana Nyankopon*, which some maintain is related to the word for
rainbow, *nyankonton*.

95. Important chiefs all have their specially trained drummers who use set proverb-
based patterns and forms to praise the chief, announce the arrival of a chief, or announce
that someone has died.

of the *mmenta* and the *sanku*.[96]
For none may look on his glory.
    None may see him with naked eyes.
Angels play their *nsankuten*,[97]
    while northerners play their *nnonno*.
All the new converts are dancing
    and singing praises to Jesus.
Let them not strain their eyes to view
    the glory that no eye can see.

The pastors are coming to town!
    They come to talk about Jesus.
No one must do them any harm
    or attempt to stand in their way.
They can never be overcome.
    The Lord holds lightning in his hand
as he leads his priests through the crowd.
    Those who attempt to do them harm
are instantly struck by lightning,
    which batters their bodies to dust
that is blown away by the wind.

There are some who seek to harm them.
    They are stubborn and determined.
They stand firm in opposition.
    They think that nothing can stop them
as they curse[98] and denounce the priests.
    They make use of evil spirits,
fetish rings,[99] idols, and needles,[100]

96. A guitar-like instrument.

97. Many large, guitar-like instruments.

98. Cursing is considered a deadly spiritual assault by the peoples of Africa—not simply the use of foul language. Words have power. In earlier times, when a person was to be executed, the executioner (*obrafo*) would put a small knife (*sapow*) through both cheeks to transfix the tongue of the condemned person, so that he would not be able to curse anyone.

99. Powerful "medicine men" and shrine custodians often wear special rings to protect themselves from spiritual harm or to use them to harm others.

100. The pins, nails, and sharp objects that are sometimes used by "witch doctors"

harmful medicine and witchcraft.
When the pastors turn to face them
in the holy name of Jesus,
a great wind will cut them in half.
Its name, *Atorom Akwasi*[101]—
the Great Power that has no name.
Let us all shout a big "amen"!

Yerebebo Obonsam adapaa![102]
We are hooting at the devil.
I do not admire the devil.
For him, only scorn do I have.
But that is not why I am here.
I want to say why I hate him.
If you should worship the devil,
to what thing shall I compare you?
To a piece of roasted plantain![103]

The devil has no love for prayer—
least of all when he hears "amen"!
Give him a very loud hooting![104]
If you follow him, you will burn
like a piece of roasted plantain.
Does that person who follows him—
the one who follows the devil—
think he is safe and living well?
The fool does not know where he is!
He is sitting on a brazier,
roasting on a charcoal fire.
When you roast plantain on charcoal,
turning it over and over

(*akomfo*) to pierce an object that represents an intended victim.

101. Nicknames, or bynames, are often used in place of the real names of dangerous entities because even pronouncing the name of powerful beings can bring harm to the speaker.

102. "We are going to disgrace the devil."

103. Plantain roasted over a hot charcoal fire is a favorite snack.

104. Scornful and derisive shouting used to show disapproval or to disgrace a person.

until it is fully roasted,
its name is called *borodedwo*.
    This *borodedwo* journeys through hell
before it is ready to eat.

They gossiped and lied about you.
    Their murmuring made you afraid.
So you consulted the fetish,
    and now their murmur is a roar.
The *osisiriw* tree has fallen
    on top of the soft *onwama*.
One is weaker than the other.
    They both will plummet together!
The devil looks out for himself.
    Will he care in the least for you?
Both of you will fall together.
    Neither one can help the other.
A drunkard leans on a thorn tree,
    and all of his body is torn
with gashes, cuts, and abrasions.
    Can someone find gold or kente
inside the grave of Ananse?[105]
    If you try this, you must be mad.
There is no gold or kente there.

Can you get sweet-smelling perfume
    from the *fitikokonini*?
It has never taken a bath.
    From birth it has lived in the dirt.
Can a lizard give you skin cream?
    Its thick hide is ragged and rough.
Can you get beautiful clothing
    from one called *okwaterekwa*?[106]
He is so poor he is naked!
    Hear his name and judge for yourself!

105. Ananse (full name: Kwaku Ananse) is an Akan folk hero and the recurrent subject of Akan folklore, or *Anansesem*.

106. A naked person.

Would you try to borrow money
   from someone who sits in prison
for not paying a paltry debt
   of just three shillings[107] and sixpence?[108]
He has recently been discharged.
   It was only four days ago.
Do you think he can help you now?
   Will you ask for a ten-pound[109] loan?
You are on a fool's errand.

Can someone with no place to stay
   offer to give you a palace
with more than a hundred guest rooms?
   He has no place to lay his head.
How will he give you a palace?

Someone says that he will give you
   some powerful black medicine.[110]
He says that after you use it,
   when you meet a snake on the path,
have no fear that it can harm you.
   But if you meet that green mamba,[111]
I beg you to run for your life!
   If you think you are free from harm,
they will bring home a silent corpse.
   Go tell this person called "someone"
that a lizard bit his father,[112]

107. Thirty cents. A Ghanaian shilling (*siren*) is ten cents.

108. Six cents. The total: thirty-six cents.

109. In colonial times, Ghana used British currency. A British pound is popularly viewed as two US dollars. Ghana's basic monetary unit is the cedi (from the Akan word for cowrie shell). But, to this day in rural areas, this basic monetary unit is still referred to as a "pound" (*pon*).

110. "Medicine" is used by practitioners both to cure and to cause harm. Harmful "medicine" is often referred to as "black medicine."

111. The green mamba is an extremely aggressive and highly poisonous snake in the forested parts of Ghana.

112. Practitioners of traditional medicine, like *malams* and "medicine men," are very secretive about their herbal formulas and the specific shrines to which they are attached.

and it left him lying there dead.

You cannot joke with the devil.
      All of his debts he will give you.
The load he will put on your head
      will be more than a person can bear.
Look at Satan and his servants
      wandering there in the desert.
Scorched by the sun, they are thirsty.
      They are chased and beaten with canes.
They are clamoring and wailing.
      Listen, all of you who can hear:
Cry out to Jesus! Do it now!
      Tell him to come to your rescue,
or an endless death awaits you.

Let us, then, all go to Jesus.
      Every good thing awaits us there.
He, the source of all that is good,
      will give us everything we need.

Those he has bathed and anointed,
      his subjects and his ministers,
are fed with the bread from heaven.
      They drink from a bottomless well
to quench an unquenchable thirst.
      No golden moons deck their foreheads;[113]
no necklace[114] of stars on their necks.
      The amazing words of Jesus
make them shine and glimmer like stars.

Even though they are far away,
      they appear like the rising sun.
Their clothing sparkles and glistens.

They pass these formulas on to one of their children only on their deathbed.

    113. The headdress of a chief is covered with golden symbols, including stars and moons.

    114. Gold necklaces and royal pendants are worn by chiefs and persons of high rank.

Their kingly robes color the sky.
Their gems and golden ornaments
    eclipse the sun with their beauty.
The kings are coming to Jesus.
    They come to greet their only King.
In worship, they fall on their knees
    face down and prostrate before him.
This is how the kings adore him.
    What a Great King this Jesus is!
When he comes, even kings bend down
    to worship him and adore him.

Have you ever seen mighty kings
    kneel down and worship the devil?
When the devil comes to visit,
    he brings a bag of misfortune:
atiridii[115] and sudden deaths,[116]
    nsamanwaw,[117] *nkonkon,*[118] *ntoburo,*[119]
snakebite, and blackwater fever.[120]
    No great kings line up at his throne
to praise him for these misfortunes.
    We have never heard their praises;
only their cries of scorn and pain.

What kind of chiefs are gathered here?
    What kind of gathering is this?
Look! Thousands of dazzling chiefs!

---

115. Malaria remains the biggest killer in Ghana. In precolonial times up until the 1960s, half of all children died of malaria and waterborne diseases before the age of five. The life of a child from birth to five years is considered very tentative. Women will often say, "I gave birth to ten but three are there [have stayed]." The others died in infancy.

116. "Unexpected deaths," or "bad death," refers to any death before old age and is usually considered a curse. It prevents those who have died such deaths from becoming an ancestor.

117. Tuberculosis.

118. Whooping cough.

119. Smallpox.

120. A collapse of the liver caused by chronic malaria—named for the color of the urine.

The priests and the pastors have come.
They show Jesus to the nations!
    It is a glorious durbar[121]
calling the kings to assemble.
        They come to glorify his name
and receive his many blessings.
        It is not for us commoners
that these mighty kings assemble.
            Only for Jesus, our Sovereign.

When you walk the path of Jesus,
        your eyes will see amazing things.
You will see his glorious kings—
        the pomp and grandeur of his chiefs
who stand before him in glory.[122]
        In the past, we did not know them.
But now, because of Jesus' name,
        we go to greet his kings at dawn,[123]
to meet them in all their glory.
            We are all exceedingly blessed!

On our way to this assembly,
        we carried nothing in our hands.
Jesus has filled our empty arms
        with a bountiful load of gifts.
He brings his giant bulldozer
        to haul our massive load away.

Jesus is the Enchanted Well.
        When women drink of its water,
a year later when they return,

---

121. A British colonial term of Hindi derivation (*darbar*) denoting a grand celebration with sumptuary displays of power and grandeur for the king. They were regularly held in Ghana by the Asante chief (*Asantehene*), who in precolonial times exercised considerable control over the West African geography that is now Ghana.

122. On solemn occasions, chiefs and their courtiers are lavishly adorned with expensive clothing and gold.

123. Important meetings and discussions are traditionally held early in the morning.

they carry babies at their backs![124]
This well is the life of Jesus
and the water of life, his word.
When you put your faith in his word,
hold it close, and grow it with prayer,
so fruitful will your womb become
and so plentiful your children,[125]
their abundance will wear you out!
No one is able to count them!
We will never need more children![126]
Let us all shout a big "amen"!

Jesus, the Elephant Hunter,
hunts elephants to feed his priests.
When he takes his gun to the bush,
he hunts the biggest of the lot.
He needs only to aim his gun,
and meat is there on the table.
He is the Butcher with Muscles!
He serves up huge portions of meat.
His cutlass chops up giant bulls.
Young men rush over with baskets
to take the carcasses away.
He tells the priests to keep us fed
until we have all had our fill.
All the nations flock to Jesus.
All the people come to be fed.
To Jesus they hasten and run

124. Such water is offered—by both traditional "medicine men" at their shrines and Pentecostal prophets at their "prayer camps"—to pilgrims seeking good health and special favors like pregnancy for a barren woman.

125. Children are of supreme value among the Akan. A woman who bears ten children is given the honor called *badu* (literally, "ten children") whereby she is held up as a model for the village, and a sheep is slaughtered for her and her friends to eat.

126. In village life, children are a great asset. By the time a child is six, it can produce enough to sustain one person. By twelve, a boy can sustain three. Nowadays, with the need for schooling and with half the population living in urban centers, children are more of a burden.

to gather fat portions of meat.[127]

Jesus has donned his hunter's smock.[128]
  He is going to hunt big game
for widows to have their bush meat.[129]
  He gives what is left to the poor,
to the orphans, and to the sick.

Jesus, the Greatest of Hunters,
  whose domain is the forest deep,
searches the woodlands day and night
  to find and kill *Sasabonsam*,[130]
the fearsome creature of the wild,
  and entrap the *mmoatia*,
the creature's wily servant dwarfs.[131]

He urges the youth to be firm,
  to resist the devil's deceit.
This has confounded the devil—
  made him angry and bewildered.
His devils are vexed and confused.
  Jesus has smacked down the lion
and flattened the bear with a fan;
  has crushed the hyena with a breeze
and slaughtered the fox in its den.
  Such are the things that Jesus does—
Jesus, the Strongest of Hunters!

He is the Keen-Eyed Sharpshooter
  whose gun never misses its mark.

127. There are many references to "meat" in Afua's praises because in village life meat is a rare treat.

128. The heavy outer cotton smock or jacket worn by hunters and warriors. It is covered with protective amulets.

129. Bush meat, or the meat of wild animals, is a delicacy, and nowadays it is quite rare and expensive.

130. The dangerous mythical spirit of the forest commonly associated with Satan.

131. The word "dwarfs" (*mmoatia*) refers not to people of smaller-than-normal stature but to small, mythical, mischievous creatures of the wild.

He has gone to hunt *Bomote*,[132]
 the creature that no eye can see.
It prowls the night to eat your soul
 and leaves you to die at daybreak.
By Jesus' touch, your soul is safe.
 Jesus has killed this dreadful beast!
Go to see it in the morning.
 It is lying there in the square—
in the open for all to see.
 So, let us give praise to his name!
Let us all shout, "*Mo, mo!*" "Well done!"[133]

All the nations give thanks to you—
 the one whose gun never misses.[134]
The soul-eating beast, *Bomote*,
 has been slain by the Hunter's gun.
Let Jesus, the Hunter, be praised!
 Whenever Jesus passes by,
I implore you, please let me know.
 Show him to me or point him out,
for his name is unknown to me.
 Please, come and tell me where he is,
so that I can go to meet him.
 For this life of mine is not good.
A bitterness overwhelms me.
 Torment and anguish are my lot.
We sit here mumbling useless words.
 We say, "Never mind, never mind,"
when all the people of our house
 are dying, one by one, each day—
dying to the very last one![135]

---

132. A mythical monster. A large species of lizard (possibly monitor lizard), the subject of mythical projections.

133. *Mo* ("well done") is an expression of tribute.

134. Hunting with the old flintlock rifles is dangerous because the flints do not always spark and the odd pieces of metal and stone that are often used as bullets do not fly straight.

135. One person dying after another in the same family, starting with the most junior and delicate, and ending with the most senior. It is a sign of an ancestor's curse. Each one

I want to find shelter in him—
      to bathe in the blood of Jesus
and be saved by his sacred blood.
      Without Jesus' blood, we are lost.
I turned to the left and the right,
      looked out to the east and the west,[136]
but saw no one there to save us.
      No one can save us but Jesus!
We are waiting for him to come,
      to fight for us and redeem us.

See him there at the battlefront—
      there where he stalks our enemies.
Let us get up and go to him.
      We will not wait for another.
He is the only one who saves.
      Long ago, he fought to save us.
He is fighting to save us still.
      Let us not sit and wait for him.
He is already here with us—
      here, leading his warriors on.

Let us go over to meet him.
      Let us go to be at his side.
Do you see someone from the east
      hurrying here to redeem us?
Are you still waiting for someone
      to come from the west to save us?
You need not wait any longer
      for someone to come and redeem.
Jesus Christ has already come
      to die for us and redeem us.

---

is "called" to the court of the ancestors to account for an injustice in the family or the breaking of a taboo imposed by an ancestor. When it is discovered through a diviner, it must be addressed, or the deaths will continue until everyone in the family has gone to be judged.

    136. The four corners of the world are God's domain. He leads the fight against the devil and rescues us.

See him there at the battlefront.
    Go to the front and be with him.
Rush up to be there at his side.
    For Jesus is the chosen one
who died for us to redeem us.

He, the General of the camp,
    is our Champion in battle.
Let us get up and stand by him!
    There is a River inside him—
one that flows with milk and honey.
    It is a Powerful River
that growls with a thunderous roar.
    He, the River, holds up his gun[137]
as he leads his priests and pastors.
    All are there inside this River—
all surrounded by brilliant stars.
    Lightning is there at the center.
It rumbles and brightly flashes.
    Fire shoots out from the center.
The sun defends us from the front;
    the moon defends us from behind.

The River gushes from a Rock—
    the Cornerstone on Temple Mount.
It flows with the blood of Jesus.
    If you go to drink of this Font,
everlasting life will be yours.
    You may not drink of this River
without permission of the priests.
    First, you must go to the pastors,
who will wash you and anoint you.[138]
    Only then will they permit you.

---

137. A reference to the loud fire-belching, muzzle-loading "Dane guns," or flintlock rifles, that are still in use among Akan hunters.

138. Holy water, or blessed water, is often used by the Akan in the same way that "medicine water" is used by traditional practitioners—both for bathing and for drinking.

But if you go without their say,[139]
　　　the glory of his holy blood
will burn your body to ashes.

Tell me why it is that the priests
　　　are themselves not burnt by this flood?
Jesus anointed them with oil.
　　　They are the servants of the flood.

Jesus is a Royal River.
　　　He is greatly honored and loved,
clear as crystal in a mirror
　　　and three times as broad as the sea.
It cannot flow over the land.
　　　If it were to flow on the land,
the whole planet would be covered.
　　　All depths and valleys would be filled.
No hills or mountains would be seen—
　　　just living water everywhere.

The priests adjusted their head pads
　　　to bear the River on their heads.
At times, it becomes a Great Wind
　　　that encircles and guards the priests.
It will not blow over the land.
　　　Were it to rage across the land,
forests would be ripped from the earth
　　　and would be cast into the sea.
It circulates above the earth
　　　and protects the nations below.

At times, it becomes a fire
　　　that surrounds the pastors and priests.
It burns with fearsome violence,
　　　but its fury does them no harm.
It does not touch the countryside.

139. Strong medicines and amulets have the power both to heal and to harm. They
can even harm the "medicine man" if not used with the permission of the shrine spirit.

Were it to rage across the land,
the fury of this blazing storm
  would reduce the world to ashes.

If you merely touch the pastors,
  your body will burn to ashes!
Do not put your hand in fire!
  Never attempt to do them harm.
They are the ones he has chosen.
  They have been sent here by Jesus.
They have come here to bring his word.
  Those who hear his word and believe
have fullness of life forever—
  the blessings that were promised us.
When you turn your ear to his priests,
  you will be filled with his blessings.
If you believe, then shout, "Amen!"

Why are pastors there in the towns?
  The River told them to go there.
He has called each of them by name.
  They have all been called by Jesus
to be a light for the nations.
  He sent them here to preach his word—
his saving word—to the people.
  Whether it is for a *malam*,
a fetish priest, or soothsayer—
  who, though weak, can easily kill—
or a dangerous armed robber,
  or adulterous deceiver,
the pastors preach to everyone,
  and those who listen will be saved.

I overheard a great man speak.
  I went up to him to listen.
It was then that I heard the word.
  Priests and pastors were preaching it.
With brilliant stars leading the way,

they were preaching to the nations,
announcing the kingdom of God.
  They said that his kingdom is near.
The heavy *kontonkurowi*[140]
  covers them like a canopy,
giving protection from above.
  The rose-colored rays of sunset
safeguard the pastors from below.

As we nimbly walk toward Jesus,
  he climbs into his bulldozer
to clear away the obstacles,
  so that feet may never stumble
or be hurt on the rocky ground.

As we traveled that fearful road,
  his bright-winged angels soared above.
When robbers tried to block our path,
  they had hardly taken a step
when blindness robbed them of their sight!

When the plotters tried to kill us,
  they stood there frozen in their tracks.
A lion[141] was there to greet them.
  When they turned and tried to escape,
a green mamba was there to meet them.
  If you mean to harm the pastors,
you will only meet grief and pain.
  The priests are there to protect us.
We are safe when we are with them.

---

140. The halo of haze that surrounds a full moon which is caused by high humidity.

141. Lions feature in Akan proverbs and folklore as the most powerful and most feared of all wild animals.

Some time ago, I dreamt[142] of bulls—
    brutal bush cows—following me.
When I tried to escape the threat,
    I was covered in angry clouds.
I struggled in them till daybreak—
    without any sleep until dawn.
Whenever I laid on my bed,
    the sleep that I sought ran away.
My bones were weak with sleeplessness.
    Tiredness tried to leave me dead.

But now, all my troubles are gone.
    Let all say, "Thanks be to Jesus!"
The day that I came to believe—
    the day the pastors baptized me;
it was ten years ago today—
    since that day, the dark clouds have gone.
Bush cows have vanished from my dreams.
    From six o'clock in the evening
until seven in the morning,
    without a break of any kind,
I sleep in the peace of the Lord—
    no longer troubled by such dreams.
For this, I am thankful to God
    and sing my praises to Jesus.

Jesus, you are the Mighty Tree,[143]
    the Monarch of the Deep Forest
that hovers over the crossroads.[144]
    Your boughs offer refreshing shade
for travelers to take their rest,
    to ease their load and cool their hearts.
You offer your trunk to lean on.

142. In dreams, the soul is believed to wander about. It can be attacked and destroyed in this state by spiritual forces, causing the body to waste away.

143. Most of the rain forests of southern Ghana have been harvested.

144. Crossroads are nexus points with the unseen world.

Jesus, you are the Mighty Rock,[145]
> a Great Monument to guide us.
A Hopeful Sign at the crossroads,
> you point us in your direction—
the way to everlasting life—
> so pilgrims may not lose their way
or take the path that leads to death.

Amazed by your love, I bend low.
> Your very own body you give.
It is torn by sharp devices
> and is bruised by hatred and lies.
You, the source of all that is good—
> with a thorny crown I greet you.
It is willingly worn by you—
> the Humble Lamb I lead to death
and Lauded Lamb who brings us life.
> His death cross gave us his Spirit.
His Spirit has given us life.

In times past, with weapons and might
> they rode their horses to Zion.
They journeyed to find a prophet—
> their leper leader to wash clean.
But now, the blood of Jesus cleans.
> When you go to your room to pray,
before you reach that inner door,
> the leper inside you is clean.

Jesus, you are River Afram.
> You are the great *Wusi-amee*.[146]
Your waters provide us with meat—
> the liver of crocodile!
Your waters supply us with fish—

145. Prominent monoliths—like Bruku, an earth shrine near Kwahu-Tafo—are thought to be connecting points between the seen and unseen worlds. They are the dwelling places of "earth spirits." In the Old Testament, we find the same references to earth shrines in high places such as Tabor, El Shaddai, and Sinai.

146. The name of the Afram River's spirit.

huge crabs and catfish you offer.
Oh *Nwii* and *Asubone*,[147]
    you give us water for cooking.
Oh *Werempem Adu Afram*,[148]
    you give us fishes, big and small.
Mpasua and *Kyekyebon*,[149]
    you allow us to eat your crabs.

You are the Primeval Forest
    that furnishes us with bush meat.
You are the Replanted Forest,
    from which we harvest giant snails.[150]
You are all the Minor Rivers,
    which give us small freshwater crabs.
Jesus, you are the Deep Forest,
    from which we harvest elephants,
huge hippos, and fat wild boar.

Jesus, you, the River *Senkyi*,
    send tilapia and hippos.
You leave us shellfish on the rocks
    and invite us to eat the flesh
of *apese* and *kotoko*.[151]
    You are the Greatest of Rivers.
You feed us hunks of hippo.

No kin of mine is a hunter.
    Jesus is our only Hunter.
He calls us to come and collect
    our portions of elephant meat—
he, the Hunter of Elephants.

Of fishermen kin, I have none.

147. Two rivers in Asante-Kwahu geography.
148. Nickname for the Afram River.
149. Two small streams in the Asante-Kwahu area.
150. Giant snails are a delicacy among the Akan.
151. Hedgehog and porcupine.

Jesus, the Sea Hawk, [152] hooks our fish,
then drops them into our baskets—
      the baskets that give us our life.

When you go to visit Jesus,
      no need for a pillow or bed.
So bright the light in Jesus' house
      that nightly shadows never fall.
No need for sleep or pillowed bed.
      Let us all say a big "amen"!

All of us have had our problems,
      have had to face dangers and death.
But amazing things have happened—
      unexpected and wonderful!
Let us tell Jesus about it!
      Once, we chanced upon a lion.
When we ran away in terror,
      a deadly green mamba appeared.

Tell Jesus that we are captives.
      We are locked in a hollow tree.[153]
Two cutlasses[154] hang overhead.
      Overwhelmed are we by our plight.
Let him extend his saving hand.
      Only his saving hand can help.
There is no need for him to come.
      Let him merely extend his hand,
then all our troubles will vanish.

Long before our prayer has ended,
      long before our message is sent—
it is hardly out of our mouths
      when Jesus, with an outstretched arm,
has demolished the devil's house,

152. Osprey.

153. Baobab trees often have hollowed-out insides that are quite roomy.

154. Cutlasses, or machetes, were standard equipment for an Akan warrior.

destroyed his evil plans and deeds,
scattered his army of plotters,
        hunted them down and captured them,
and smashed them to bits and pieces,
        like shattered fragments of iron,
which he sweeps up and throws away.

Is this the meat of elephants
        that lies there in bloody pieces?
It looks like a busy playground
        of houseflies and buzzing blue flies
dancing joyfully on their prize.
        No, it is our own dancing feet
that, by the might of Jesus' blood,
        are prancing on the devil's corpse
like dancing kings at a durbar.

If you want the help of Jesus,
        just ask him to stretch out his hand.
Not for Jesus himself to come—
        he need only extend his hand
along with wonderful deeds.
        Then you will see us as victors
performing our victory dance.

When Jesus touches the devil,
        his evil kingdom is destroyed.
But when he touches his people,
        you will see them shining like stars.
Jesus' touch is like a cannon.
        When he points it at the devil,
an explosion sends destruction,
        a barrage of fiery shells.
When he stretches his blowtorch hand,
        it ignites a raging fire,
belching black and billowing smoke
        that turns Satan into a cinder.
Not one of his devils survive!

Sasabonsam and his genies—
      they were the first to be roasted.
Then, one by one, the devils burnt!
      When again he stretched out his hand,
the devil's fortress was shattered
      into a thousand blackened shards.

The frantic devil has gone mad,
      has fallen from his dizzy heights
to be crushed by *Katapilla.*
      Jesus stretched his frightful arm,
and we could hear the cannon roar.
      Satan has been ground to powder
like flour on a grinding stone.
      Let us all say a big "amen"!

Glossary

aberantekuw: A group of youth or warriors.

abodin: Praise titles.

adehyekasa: The speech style of those who belong to the royal family.

adurufo: A medicine man, a local practitioner of magic medicine.

aduwuro: A handheld iron gong hit with a stick and used to make announcements.

Afram: The main river of the Afram plains in eastern Asante, north of Kwahu.

Akan: The overall name of the many different Twi-speaking peoples of Ghana.

akpeteshi: An alcoholic drink distilled from palm wine.

Afua: The Akan name for someone born on Friday. Ghanaians use "day names."

amoma: The poetic form of language used by chiefs.

Ananse: A reference to the Asante folk hero Kwaku Ananse (literally, "spider").

Anansesem: Asante folktale with Kwaku Ananse as the hero.

ananwonam: A person who presents himself as important but is not.

anibue: Refers to the influence the West has had on Africa (literally, "Get your eyes opened").

apese: Hedgehog.

Asante: The most powerful and important of all the Akan peoples.

Asantehene: The highest-ranking chief, or king, of the Asante.

Asubone: A river in the Asante-Kwahu area.

atiridii: Fever or malaria.

Atorom Akwasi: The "Sunday" day name for *Atorom*, an unmentionable monster.

atumpan: A large type of drum played in pairs.

badu: An honor given to an Asante woman who has borne ten children.

bobo: Name for a deaf person.

Bomote: A mythical monster; also a species of lizard, possibly monitor lizard.

borodedwo: A Twi word for roasted plantain.

Bruku: A monolithic "earth shrine" on the Kwahu Plateau near Kwahu-Tafo.

bush cow: The dangerous African "Cape buffalo."

cedi: The basic unit of Ghanaian currency (literally, "cowrie shell").

Dane guns: Flintlock rifles traded from Danish merchants in precolonial times.

dunsinni: A herbalist or one who uses natural remedies to heal.

durbar: A formal assembly to mark a state or royal occasion (Hindi: *darbar*, court).

Eye nwonwa!: "It is amazing!"

fetish: A generic name for any African spiritual power, their shrines, and their custodians.

fitikokonini: Asante word for antlion (scientific name: *myrmeleontidae*).

Hweoo!: An expression of amazement ("Look at that!").

kasa a emu do: Language that is deep or profound.

katapilla: Bulldozer, from Caterpiller Inc., a company that produces large industrial equipment.

kente: A prestigious and costly cloth woven on traditional narrow looms.

Konkrompe: A massive junkyard with machinery and repair shops in Kumasi.

kontonkurowi: Byname for a dense fog in Ghana's forested lowlands.

kotoko: Porcupine.

Kristo: Christ.

Kuma: Usually added to a "day name" (literally, "little," "lesser," "junior").

Kwaebirentuw Ase Yesu: The Twi version of *Jesus of the Deep Forest*.

Kwaforomoah Takyi: Chimpanzee with the personal byname, "Tekyi," i.e., Tekyi the Chimp.

Kwahu: A Twi-speaking people and a mountainous area east of Asante.

Kyekyebon: Small stream in the Asante-Kwahu area.

malam: A Muslim marabout or itinerant cleric.

mfirikyiwa: A type of musical instrument.

*mmeakas*a: The speech style of women.

mmebusem: Proverbs and parables.

mmenta: Stringed instruments.

mmeran: Honorable attributes.

mmoatia: Mythical figures living in the forest, commonly called "dwarfs" (literally, "little animals").

Mo: An expression of praise, like "Good!" "Great!" "You have done well!"

mpanyin kasa: The speech style of elders.

Mpasua: A small stream in the Asante-Kwahu area.

Nana Nyankopon: A gentler, nonauthoritarian image of God (literally, "Grandfather God").

nkonkon: Whooping cough.

nnawuta: An instrument used to announce an important event or person.

nnonno: Small hourglass-shaped drums used in northern Ghana.

nsamanwaw: Tuberculosis.

nsankuten: Many big stringed instruments.

ntoburo: Smallpox.

Nwii: A river in the Asante-Kwahu area.

Nyame dua: A shrine for offerings to God (literally, "God's tree").

nyankonton: Rainbow.

Nyankopon: The most important name for God.

nyanno: The chief's drummers.

obabarima: A byname (literally, a "woman man") for a strong-minded postmenopausal woman.

oba-barima: A byname (literally, "woman-man") for a pair of drums with higher and lower tones.

obokasa or *opokasa*: Courteous or polite speech style.

Obonsam: An entity commonly interpreted as Satan.

obrafo: The Asante executioner.

oburoni koko: European or "white man" (literally, "red man from over the horizon").

Odo nsa da: A reference to giving things in threes, meaning "Love never ends".

odo: A large catfish and favorite food among the Asante.

okomfo: The custodian of an "earth shrine" or idol.

okuruakwaban: A person of great strength.

okwaterekwa: A naked person.

okyeame: The royal spokesperson who interprets for chiefs.

onwama: A forest tree in Ghana with soft wood and unsuitable for building.

osisiriw: A forest tree in Ghana with strong, hard wood.

palanquin: A litter or a conveyance to carry a person, adopted from Hindi.

pesewa: An old copper coin modeled on the British twopence.

pito: A beer in norhern Ghana made from sorghum or millet.

pon: Pound, a British unit of currency.

Sakyi: A byname for a dense fog in the forested lowlands.

sankofa: A trend in the 1970s to revalue African traditions (literally, "Go back and get it").

sanku: A stringed instrument.

sapow: A small, sharp knife used by executioners to pierce the tongue and prevent a curse.

Sasabonsam: A mythical spirit of the forest commonly identified with Satan.

Sebe: "Please excuse what I am about to say."

Senkyi: A river in Ghana known for rapids and waterfalls.

siren: Ghanaian shilling.

Tigare: The name of a particular shrine from northern Ghana which catches witches.

Tutu Ampa: A mythical figure of great power.

Twea!: An expression for contempt.

Twi: The language of the Akan peoples.

Werempem Adu Afram: A byname for the Afram River.

Wusi-amee: The name of the Afram River's spirit.

Yaa Asantewaa: The Asante queen-mother warrior of Ejisu (1840–1921).

Yerebebo adapaa: Literally, "We are going to disgrace/shame [someone]."

Yesu: Jesus.

Bibliography

Bevans, Stephen B. *Models of Contextual Theology*. Maryknoll, New York: Orbis, 1992.

Christaller, J. G. *Dictionary of the Asante and Fante Language Called Tshi (Twi)*. 2nd ed. Basel, Switzerland: Basel Evangelical Missionary Society, 1933.

Fretheim, Sara J. "'Jesus! Say It Once and the Matter Is Settled': The Life and Legacy of Oral Theologian Madam Afua Kuma of Ghana (1908–1987)." *Journal of African Christian Biography* 5.3 (2020) 18–38.

Kirby, Jon P., ed. *Jesus of the Deep Forest: Prayers and Praises of Afua Kuma*. Accra, Ghana: Asempa, 1981.

———, ed. *Kwaibirentuw Ase Yesu: Afua Kuma Ayeyi ne Mpaebo*. Accra, Ghana: Asempa, 1981.

———. *The Power and the Glory: Popular Christianity in Northern Ghana*. Trends in African Christianity. Akropong-Akuapem, Ghana: Regnum Africa, 2013.

Rahner, Karl. "Towards a Fundamental Theological Interpretation of Vatican II." *Theological Studies* 40.4 (1979) 716–27.

CPSIA information can be obtained
at www.ICGtesting.com
Printed in the USA
JSHW012305150622
27151JS00007B/13

9 781666 730982